ARKANA

Seeing the Invisible

Born in 1925, Meg Maxwell was brought up in Kenya and read Philosophy, Politics and Economics at Oxford. She married and lived in Africa and Arabia before returning to England in 1963. She took a Postgraduate Teaching Training Certificate at London University and taught in London comprehensive schools. She returned to Oxford in 1984 and has worked for four years at the Alister Hardy Research Centre, helping to evolve a computer-assisted method of analysing the accounts of spiritual experience. She has also helped with research for a book about Kenya and has been a marriage counsellor for thirteen years. She has an extended family of children, step-children and grandchildren.

Verena Tschudin was born and brought up in Switzerland. She trained in nursing and midwifery in London, then entered a convent, where she had her first spiritual experience. On leaving the convent, she went to Jerusalem for about four years. On her return to London she continued to nurse and additionally trained as a counsellor, and it was in this capacity that she began to hear of people's spiritual experiences and to take them seriously. She studied for a BSc and now works as a counsellor for Reaching Out, a counselling and listening service based in Earl's Court, London. She writes and lectures mostly for nurses.

SEEING THE INVISIBLE

MODERN RELIGIOUS AND
OTHER TRANSCENDENT EXPERIENCES

Edited by
Meg Maxwell and Verena Tschudin

ARKANA

ARKANA

Published by the Penguin Group
Penguin Books Ltd, 27 Wrights Lane, London w8 5tz, England
Viking Penguin, a division of Penguin Books USA Inc.
375 Hudson Street, New York, New York 10014, USA
Penguin Books Australia Ltd, Ringwood, Victoria, Australia
Penguin Books Canada Ltd, 2801 John Street, Markham, Ontario, Canada l3r 1b4
Penguin Books (NZ) Ltd, 182–190 Wairau Road, Auckland 10, New Zealand

Penguin Books Ltd, Registered Offices: Harmondsworth, Middlesex, England.

First published 1990
1 3 5 7 9 10 8 6 4 2

Filmset in Ehrhardt (Linotron 202) by
CentraCet, Cambridge
Printed in England by Clays Ltd, St Ives plc

He held to his purpose as one seeing the invisible

Hebrews 11:27

Contents

*

Contents

Preface

*

The brief from the director of the Alister Hardy Research Centre (AHRC) to us as editors was to produce an edited anthology of the accounts in the collection. This was exciting and generous. The basic criterion for choice was that each account should contain an experience or experiences, and simply be the writer's own interpretation.

Armed with these two instructions, we set about our task, and that, like Topsy, 'growed and growed'. We discovered more and more facets. We devised guidelines, only to discard them; theories, and found they couldn't apply; categories, and had to abandon them. It was not until we came to look at the accounts very closely that we realized that we could not label what the writers hadn't labelled. These are accounts of *experiences*, and therefore each is totally unique, personal and completely subjective. After many trials and discussions we have decided to present the accounts by their patterns, that is, by whether the person has written of a single experience only; of one main experience and others mentioned but not detailed; or of multiple experiences. As a short chapter we have included three accounts that speak of a 'continuous awareness' rather than a clear experience. In this way we felt that we were most closely following the request for an anthology: presenting a selection of accounts, without thereby making any other statement than that which the writer herself or himself made.

We chose the accounts for the readability, variety of content, length, representation of type and appeal to either of us personally, and, we hope, to the readers.

Almost all the accounts are in the form of a letter, many of them handwritten originally. By producing them in book form, they sadly lose some of the spontaneity and personal touch. Where possible, we have not changed syntax, but have corrected spelling errors.

Names of people and places have been abbreviated to the first letter, but where identification would have been too easy, we have used a general term (i.e. 'in Greece', rather than leaving the name of the particular island).

The names of the writers of the accounts have been left out, thus maintaining anonymity. However, where possible, the age of the experient has been included: the figure at the beginning of the account signifies the age at the time of writing, and the figure in brackets is the age at which the experience happened.

The figure on the far right is the official AHRC reference number for that account.

As far as we could, we have endeavoured to contact all the writers of the accounts, and sought and obtained their permission to publish their account. In some instances we had no name, knew that the person had moved but had no new address or knew that the person had died. We hope that, should a reader of this book by chance find his or her account included without knowing about it, he or she will accept our apologies.

Because the subject is one of many aspects and facets and few definitions we have included a glossary to help readers with the more common terms used. As much as possible we have not taken over dictionary phrases, but used our own understanding of the words and that reflected by the writers of the accounts.

The title of the book was not easy to choose. We settled on *Seeing the Invisible* because in this field of otherness and religion and new dimensions a title with some paradox in it seemed not inappropriate.

We are very much aware that the experiences recorded here are all from people whose background is Western and Judaeo-Christian. Perhaps this book will help to widen the collection and the understanding of transcendence in other cultures and religions.

We wish to thank all those who have helped us, but in particular the people at the AHRC headquarters: Geoffrey Ahern, Tim Beardsworth, David Hay, Mike Jackson, Oliver Knowles, Tim Pearce, Edward Robinson and Polly Wheway. Margaret Wellings had the marathon task of typing the manuscript not only of the editors but also of the accounts, and all that this represents in deciphering handwriting. A heartfelt thank you to her. Robin

Waterfield of Arkana deserves a particular thanks for his interest and enthusiasm in this project. We are grateful to all those who helped us.

Meg Maxwell, Oxford
Verena Tschudin, London
October 1989

All proceeds of the sale of this book go to the Alister Hardy Research Centre.

The Alister Hardy
Research Centre†

*

The Alister Hardy collection of accounts represented in this anthology is unique. It is an archive of more than 5,000 accounts collected over twenty years, originally in response to the initiative of Sir Alister Hardy, biologist and, later, Professor of Zoology at Oxford. He published appeals in journals and pamphlets or gave interviews in newspapers, of which the following is one example:[1]

To further his research . . . Professor Hardy is seeking the help of *Observer* readers. [Then follows this example of the sort of thing he wanted.] 'Beatrice Webb . . . was conscious of experiencing a sense of reverence or awe – an apprehension of a power and purpose outside herself – which she called "feeling" and which was sometimes induced by appreciation of great music or corporate worship. But her experiences went further than this nebulous fleeting "feeling" – because as a result of it she achieved a religious interpretation of the universe which satisfied and upheld her and enabled her to seek continuous guidance in prayer – and this without compromising her intellectual integrity.'

Professor Hardy proposes, if readers will kindly co-operate, to study and compare as many personal records of such experiences as possible. *He invites all who have been conscious of, and perhaps influenced by, some such power, whether they call it the power of God or not, to write a simple and brief account of these feelings and their effects* [Editors' emphasis]. They should include particulars of age, sex, nationality, religious upbringing and other factors thought to be relevant. . . . They will be regarded as strictly confidential and names will be suppressed in any published accounts of the research.[2]

Over the next twenty years nearly every appeal on behalf of the research was similar to the above, giving examples and including the italicized sentence.

†. Alister Hardy Research Centre, Westminster College, North Hinksey, Oxford OX2 9AT.

This was intentionally a very broad description of what was wanted, not defining the experience as 'religious' or 'spiritual', but nevertheless tilted towards awareness of a divinity. People responded simply because they wanted to, knowing that someone was seriously interested in what they had to say. Although this personal response means that no statistically based generalizations can be made from the collection – the subjects were self-selected and not chosen for their representativeness as men or women, old or young, Protestant, Roman Catholic or other religion, agnostic or atheist – it does provide marvellously spontaneous and varied accounts, rich in subject and in variety of language, and each account expressing its own completeness at the time of writing.

What was Sir Alister Hardy's purpose in making this collection?

In order to put the answer to that question into its context we have to look back about a hundred years to the time when the idea of 'scientifically' studying religious experience first emerged. 'Scientific', in this sense, did not mean explaining everything in terms of physics or chemistry or mathematics, but rather it expressed an attitude of mind, of hoping to learn about the nature of things by carefully studying them in great detail as they are and then drawing conclusions. At the end of the last century psychology was a developing science, with depth psychologists such as Sigmund Freud studying the behaviour of individuals, drawing conclusions as to what this indicated about their minds, and developing the idea of the 'unconscious' as a psychological reality. Psychologists such as William James, Edwin Starbuck and W. T. Stace pioneered the scholarly study of personal religious experiences. William James, an American, in particular attracted widespread interest by the publication of his *The Varieties of Religious Experience* in 1902.[3] He had studied the experiences of a great many people, among them his friends, his patients, the saints, primitive people and atheists, to mention only some. He was, as he said, 'bent on rehabilitating the element of feeling', by which he meant the feelings of individuals, 'in religions and subordinating its intellectual part'.[4] Although he had never had a religious experience, he did identify in himself 'that mystical germ', as he called it, that enabled him to recognize the truth in the experiences of others. 'It is a very common germ', he wrote. 'It creates the rank and file of believers.'[5]

It was not until over sixty years later, in 1969, that Sir Alister Hardy also turned to the study of religious experiences. He was a biologist and a Darwinian who believed in the process of natural selection but was unhappy at Darwin's rather mechanical explanation. He felt that the spiritual side of mankind, much neglected by biologists, played an important part in the survival of the species. Determined to learn more about this aspect of human nature, he set to work, as a biologist would, to collect specimens, asking people to write to him of their experiences. In accordance with a still widely held view, he thought there were basically two types of religious experience and that these were what he would find: 'on the one hand those describing a more general sense of spiritual awareness, and on the other, those which were of a more dramatic, ecstatic and mystical character'.[6] He was like a fisherman casting his net upon the waters, but instead of coming up with a few well-defined fish, he found he had caught a great array of glittering creatures that did not seem to fit his preconceived grouping. Together with a team of researchers, he set to work to sort, analyse and categorize this collection. These were the basis of the present collection and thus began what has now become the Alister Hardy Research Centre in Oxford.

Alister Hardy did not find the simplicity he was looking for, but, with the assistance of Tim Beardsworth and Vita Toon, much detailed and important information came out of the study of the experiences, so much information, in fact, that it was difficult to make generalizations and draw conclusions. Much was learned in detail about such matters as how the experiences were 'sensed' or otherwise perceived; when, where and in what various circumstances; and what the contents of the experiences were. Much was also learned about the feelings that accompanied these experiences, some profound and wonderful, others anguished and fearful. It became clear that many people claimed that the experiences were unforgettable, totally changing their lives for the better, giving them new purpose and meaning, less fear of death and better relationships with others.

At that time studies were made at the Centre and books published about the large number of experiences that were described as occurring in childhood,[7] and about the 'sense of presence'[8] that was also reported with great frequency.

As a result of many of these findings, it seemed important to discover how many and what sort of people in the population were having such experiences. David Hay undertook to make surveys on behalf of the AHRC in the 1970s and 1980s.[9] His research showed that in nation-wide opinion polls, in which only the bare question 'Have you ever been conscious of a presence or power other than your everyday self?' was asked, about 33 per cent of the people said yes, and that in a Nottingham survey of 172 people, where questionnaires and follow-up interviews made the question clearer, 107 people, or 62 per cent, answered yes. Similar research in the USA produced similar results. These figures highlight the extent of the current taboo against normally acknowledging such experiences. It would be interesting to look at a busy street and to consider how many of the people there have had a spiritual experience of which they could not speak. Hay's research revealed that in Britain significantly more women than men reported religious experiences, and that experients were more likely to be church attenders. This latter fact must surely alert the Churches (of all denominations), schools and parents to the need to make religion available to children. From everything that has already been learned about these experiences it is clear that childhood is a time of spiritual openness.

The existence of this large collection of accounts at the AHRC naturally encouraged other researchers to make specialized studies. Michael Jackson is currently seeking to clarify the nature of the relationship between 'healthy' spiritual experiences and psychotic states. There is widespread fear, but also ignorance, of madness, and how it relates to spirituality, as is evident in the taboo on acknowledging religious experiences. Experiences that might be labelled 'religious' or 'spiritual' in some non-Western cultures would be seen today as madness in the materialist West – such is our present cultural conditioning. Similarities were found in the Hardy collection and elsewhere between some 'healthy' and some psychotic experiences, such as the religious imagery, other perceptual phenomena and the personally stressful circumstances at the time. One possible explanation of these similarities is that the same, possibly inheritable, personality trait could be associated with both a proneness to having healthy spiritual experiences and, in some cases, a proneness to having psychotic breakdowns. A better understanding of this relationship could have important treatment implications for psychotic conditions.

These hypotheses are not yet proven. The possibility of an inherited disposition towards spirituality is certainly controversial, but the possible linking of spiritual and psychotic states (as of artistically creative and psychotic states) is not new. James spoke of it in his first lecture[10] and, more recently, the radical British psychoanalyst R. D. Laing wrote in this connection: 'Madness need not be all breakdown. It may also be breakthrough. It is potentially liberation and renewal as well as enslavement and existential death.'[11] It is the 'breakthrough' that is interesting for the student of religious experience. In one form the breakthrough may seem to be self-induced, and is what mystics have sought (i.e. an altered state of consciousness). This is achieved for some by prayer and fasting, for others in varying ways by drugs, by music, frenzy, rhythm, chanting and many other methods, and for some, it may be psychosis. In another form the breakthrough seems to come unasked from outside, breaking through into the consciousness of the experient, which is how it often seems to be described in the accounts published here. A 'sense of the sacred' seems to depend upon some form of breakthrough in our ordinary levels of consciousness.

The tradition of analysing and comparing many accounts of religious experience, which Alister Hardy had revived, has been taken up again at the AHRC by Geoffrey Ahern, this time using computer technology to help with the process of making generalizations concerning the very wide range of variables. People reading even the 143 accounts in this book will find themselves trying to make judgements and to decide what they think these experiences mean – at least that is what we, as editors, hope they will be doing. Ahern's research employs a similar process, but at a considerably greater level of complexity and precision, avoiding the subjectivity of any one person's judgement. It entails discovering, defining and sensitively interpreting hundreds of possible meanings at several levels within each account, then using the Oxford University computer to compare, correlate and cluster these hundreds of meanings. From this computer-assisted process a wider and more reliable range of insight can be gained than could be achieved by the unassisted human mind. The aim is to achieve a clearer understanding of how men and women experience and express the profound mystery of spirituality.

Further research is already projected. In addition, the 'net' needs to be more widely flung. The accounts in the Alister Hardy Research Centre and in this book are of experiences in a basically Judaeo-Christian culture. It is certain that experience of the 'transcendent' differs in various ways between and within Western and Eastern religions and cultures. If we really believe, as Jung thought, and history seems to show, that mankind has a 'psychic aptitude' for God,[12] we could advance our understanding of this shared spirituality by studying the experiences of people living within Hindu, Muslim, Buddhist and other cultures. This could be another step forward.

An Introduction to
Transcendent Experience

*

Historical Perspectives

Experiences of other dimensions are as old as humankind. What is new about them today is the language used to describe them. Past generations lived in a more confined and slow-moving world, where the material and the spiritual, fact and fiction were not so closely defined. Today's world is fast, rational and sceptical of tradition and authority. Therefore an experience that cuts into this time and this world is startling.

Yet human nature seems always to have had or needed a spiritual aspect.[1] Archaeologists found evidence that Neanderthal man, 150,000 years ago, practised ritual burial, implying a belief in a spirit world and a life beyond the grave. Anthropologists found this awareness and its accompanying religious practices amongst all the so-called primitive peoples of the world. It seems that people have a 'feeling' for a non-material world, a faculty to experience it and a need for a god-like figure or being. In this way it is possible to make sense of life on Earth. Such ideas and abstractions have, however, to be made accessible. The leaders of the world's religions are recognized as prophets and saviours precisely because they interpreted ideas into living realities, and lived out in their lives what could not be put into words. Their visions, dreams and experiences were accepted as universally valid, and so became the symbols for all their adherents. To be part of a religious system means to be part of that experience.

Many of the religious systems and movements throughout history are based on a revelation, a vision, a dream – a 'religious experience' of one kind or another. A simple scan of some of the best-known experiences may be relevant here.

Moses, who was to lead the Israelites out of Egypt, was in the desert, looking after a flock of sheep, when he noticed a bush on fire, but not burning.[2] A voice came from the middle of the bush, asking Moses to take off his shoes because the place on which he was standing was holy (4223). Then God revealed himself to Moses as 'I am who I am' (4182). (The figures in brackets here and following refer to those printed at the beginning of each account and are the official AHRC reference numbers: see p. 215.)

In about 560 BC Siddharta Gautama, later known as the Buddha, was born in India. After much searching he came to enlightenment during three nights of contemplation. He saw his previous lives pass before him, saw with supernatural insight the cycle of birth, death and rebirth, and had revealed to him the four holy truths: the knowledge of suffering, the source of suffering, the removal of suffering and the way to the removal of suffering.[3]

The story of Jesus Christ and his call is also surrounded by supernatural experiences. The Gospel of Luke tells of encounters with angels bringing messages about Jesus to his mother, Mary, and to shepherds.[4]

Jesus' own ministry starts with his baptism in the river Jordan. After the baptism a voice came, saying 'This is my Son, the Beloved; my favour rests on him.'[5] This experience seems to have made a great impression on Jesus because he left the river to go to the desert to be alone (2476; 4267; 4278). The Gospel of Mark says that Jesus was with the wild beasts:[6] perhaps a reference to the often hard struggles to come to terms with such an experience and the consequences that may follow if they are taken seriously (2009).

The Muslim religion is similarly based on an account of how Muhammad was called.

One night in Ramadan about the year 610, as he was asleep or in a trance, the Angel Gabriel came to him and said to him: 'Recite!' He replied: 'What shall I recite?' The order was repeated three times, until the angel himself said: 'Recite in the name of your Lord, the creator, who created man from clots of blood. Recite! Your Lord is the Most Bountiful One, who by the pen has taught mankind things they did not know.'[7] (The word 'Koran' means 'recital'.)

Some of the great movements that changed history are also based on religious experiences. In 1123 Rahere, a jester at the court of King Henry I, fell ill while on pilgrimage to Rome. He

vowed that should he be allowed to return home he would found a
hospital. St Bartholomew appeared to him in a vision and bade him
found both a hospital and church in Smithfield in London. Rahere
recovered, returned home and founded St Bartholomew's Hospital,
which still stands on the same site hundreds of years later, still
caring for the sick.

Another man of high spirits, St Francis of Assisi, was also
acquainted with supernatural experiences.

High in the dark house of Assisi Francesco Benardone slept and dreamed
of arms. There came to him in the darkness a vision splendid with swords,
patterned after the cross in the crusading fashion, of spears and shields
and helmets hung in a high armoury, all bearing the sacred sign. When he
awoke he accepted the dream as a trumpet bidding him to the battle field,
and rushed out to take horse and arms.[8]

He didn't get very far before he had another dream, in which he
heard a voice saying, 'You have mistaken the meaning of the vision.
Return home.' And there, praying in the little church of San
Damiano, he heard the voice of Christ from the crucifix (4711)
saying to him: 'Go, Francis, and repair my church which is falling
into ruin.' Francis went and started repairing the church of San
Damiano, realizing only later that this message, too, was to be
understood not in a practical but in a spiritual way.

A century or so later a series of sixteen 'revelations were shown
to a simple and uneducated creature on the eighth of May 1373'.[9]
Julian of Norwich had been very ill and on the point of dying. In
and through this illness she wanted to share with Christ in his
passion, and her visions, or 'shewings', relate to the Passion and
the consequences of believing. Julian wrote with great insight and
an immediacy that makes her a favourite today. Her phrase 'All
shall be well, and all shall be well, and all manner of thing shall be
well'[10] is often quoted by experients in this collection (see p. 38).

Moving further on in history, the famous composer G. F. Handel
is associated with a transcendent experience. In the summer of
1741 he received an invitation to write the music for the oratorio
Messiah, to be performed at a charity concert in Dublin. He started
work on 22 August. One evening his servant removed the
untouched supper, noticing tears streaming down Handel's face.
He had written the 'Hallelujah' chorus with something more than

his own strength, finishing the whole work by 14 September, just twenty-three days after he began it. The practice of standing for the 'Hallelujah' chorus during a performance of the *Messiah* is perhaps a symbol of acknowledgement of the other-worldly power that made this work possible.

Nearer to our own day another well-known Church has been founded on a vision. The Church of Jesus Christ of Latter-day Saints, or Mormons, was established by Joseph Smith in 1830 after a revelation by the Prophet Mormon. This Church, with its headquarters in Salt Lake City, Utah, is well known for its charitable works – consequences of a religious experience.

The town of Lourdes in south-west France owes its reputation to an appearance of the Virgin Mary. Bernadette Soubirous had an experience in which the Virgin Mary revealed herself, and although Bernadette was disbelieved at first, she held to the authenticity of her vision. She was canonized in 1933 and the cures that continue to take place at Lourdes are a testimony to her faith.

Visions of the Virgin Mary are well documented; the shrines at Mary Knoll in Ireland and Medjugorje in Yugoslavia are of more recent origin. This latter place has become famous through TV and radio documentaries.

Transcendent experiences are particularly associated with times of stress and turmoil (see p. 31). Conflicts and wars (947; 4068) are therefore often associated with religious experiences. The 'Angel of Mons' became a fabled figure in the First World War.[11]

The early climbers of the Eiger's north face saw one of their colleagues fall to his death, and at that moment saw a luminous cross in the sky.

After the disaster at the Hillsborough stadium, Sheffield, on 15 April 1989, there were accounts in the press of premonitions of death, dreams and the miraculous deliverance of some spectators.

Churches, castles and monasteries often have legends surrounding them, basing their foundation and siting on an experience – a vision, a dream or a command. Many of these places were also associated with ghosts, but more often with springs and rivers to which cures are attributed. These sites are testimony to the beliefs of earlier generations and of their expressions and language. The disasters at Hillsborough and elsewhere have shown that people still need shrines and rituals, but now a fence may be an altar, and a pop song replace a litany whose words have become irrelevant to today's language and expressions.

What is a Transcendent Experience?

It is possible to describe an operation in terms of the organ removed, the kind of incision made, the type of anaesthetic used and the duration of the whole procedure. But this does not say anything about who the patient was and how this operation affected his or her life, health, family or work. In the same way it is possible to say certain things about the function of transcendent experiences, but this does not at all convey what went on in the person and what value that person placed on the experience.

One experient wrote:

I think that people who have experienced visions and clarities tend to try to put them in familiar words and images and these words reveal their backgrounds, but perhaps aren't right about the vision itself. When part of the vision is revealing 'how things work', what comes across is 'the machine' and then people describe gears and cogwheels and hums of motors. (2366)

This chapter is dealing mainly with the 'gears' and 'wheels', so as to put the experiences into a framework, the 'body' (to continue the car metaphor), but what counts is the person who finally drives this motor. What counts is the experience itself, not what each individual aspect of it is. But to understand the *whole*, both the external 'pieces' and the internal event have to be considered.

In an interview Lev Gillet gave the following answer to the question 'What criteria would you apply to a religious phenomenon?':

I think you have a religious phenomenon when you have, firstly, the awareness of a reality which transcends you: something bigger than yourself, something beyond your own limits. And secondly, although it is transcendent, it must in some way be immanent to yourself. And thirdly, between these two expressions of a supreme reality there is a possibility of dynamic exchange. You receive something from it and you give something to it.[12]

In another interview Martin Israel answered the question 'What exactly *is* a religious experience?' thus:

I would say that [a] religious experience is an experience of that which transcends the individual and makes him a fuller individual, which makes the personality more integrated in terms of understanding his place in the world; an experience that there is something outside him, of which he has been made aware, that broadens his view of life, something that gives him a widened awareness, and brings him to thoughts of deity. It comes spontaneously; it is not intellectually induced. This could include aspects of psychic experience. I am sure there is a difference between religious and ordinary psychic experience, but I don't think it would be wise to draw an artificial dividing line. The religious includes the psychical, but the psychical does not necessarily include the religious.[13]

Many of the people who have written accounts of their experiences have tried to answer their own questions as to what this phenomenon *is*. After describing her experience, one person added:

I have had similar experiences from time to time. I can only describe them as an opening of a window, or the lifting of a corner of a curtain. They are always brief, not more than a flash, and the effect, or the glimpse they give of something more real than obvious reality, lasts forever. Perhaps it is a feeling akin to (. . .) the highest reaches of art and music? I do not know. I am capable of being profoundly moved by music, painting, poetry, literature, plays . . . but these rare 'illuminations' go further than emotion. (4693)

In an effort to give a name to these experiences, thereby defining them, several terms have been put forward:

religious,
mystical,
numinous,[14]
transcendent,
prophetic,[15]
peak.[16]

James coined the expression 'religious experience' in his lectures at Edinburgh in 1901–2.[17] The more acceptable term today seems to be transcendent experience because, as Israel points out above, all such experiences are of a different order of knowledge, but not all are to do with religion, or at least institutional religion.

'Mystical' experiences are characterized by a sense of union (see p.24) and 'numinous' experiences by a sense of the presence of God (see p.33). There is often overlap, or both aspects happen in the same experience, but equally often they are quite distinct – at least in the accounts sent to the AHRC.

The word 'prophetic' (947) is used mostly of the type of experience that includes visions and voices after the manner of the prophets of the Bible. 'Prophetic' could be a misleading word and we therefore use the word 'visionary' to cover this type of experience (see p.28).

Abraham Maslow created the term 'peak experiences' to include a wide range of the more ecstatic transcendent experiences. An important study of such experiences was also made by Marghanita Laski.[18]

The Taboo

Before going further we need to acknowledge the fact that many of the people who have these experiences find it very difficult to speak about them. There is a widely felt taboo on the subject. Several reasons for this are given by the writers of the accounts:

- The experience is very personal. It is a secret in that person's life, and talking about it takes away that 'specialness'; it diminishes the secret and the person (4113; 4230; 4693).
- The experience is holy. It is something that should not be exposed (2848; 4422; 4267).
- The experience is so totally different from everyday life and realities that the experients fear being mad (4182) or a 'nut case' (2643) or 'menopausal' (4755). The fear of being regarded as different, mad, out of one's mind or talking airy-fairy nonsense is a strong one. Many people have written as strongly as they could that they are just ordinary people (143; 4315) and not given to visions (139) or hallucinations (4410). The defence that people need to make on their own behalf seems often amazingly strong.
- Some people have spoken of their experiences to one or two trusted people and were rebuffed, and therefore never again dared to mention it. This was particularly painful if the person spoken to was a minister of the Church (4248).
- The experience is so special that the person who recounts it must feel that it is acceptable. If the hearers are not directly hostile, but not sympathetic either (4278), this diminishes the experience and the experient.

Another factor is the possibility of 'giving people the shivers' (4465), which seems connected to the fear of witchcraft or occult practices and even to the ordinary psychic phenomena of clairvoyance, telepathy and precognition.

At a different psychological level people now feel that they must be able to explain everything 'scientifically'. The thinkers of the Age of Enlightenment – Newton, Copernicus and Galileo – had reached high levels of practical and intellectual understanding of the physical world. It seems that today people still regard that science as their yardstick, seeing material things as the only reality and feeling that any experience that does not fit into this framework must be explained as 'something you have eaten' or 'all in the mind'. Modern science, however, has moved on in leaps and bounds and is no longer tied to philosophical materialism. The study of transcendent experiences may indeed help to bridge that gap, bringing science and people's everyday lives together in a new understanding.

Common Elements of Religious and Other Transcendent Experiences

James describes four elements as characteristic of mystical states: there is an ineffability about them (they cannot be adequately described); a noetic quality is present (a sense of 'knowing' of a different order); there is transiency (the experience is short-lived); and there is passivity (the experience is received and happens despite what the person is doing at the time).[19] These characteristics apply largely to all types of transcendent experiences, not just the mystical. An outline of the first and third of James's characteristics (ineffability and transiency) as well as a number of other common elements is useful here.

Ineffability

Religious and transcendent experiences are of an order that we know very little about. It is not surprising, therefore, that we have not enough or not adequate language to describe what is happening. The experience is of such a sublime character that words are far too limiting. Those who struggle to put into words what they experienced invariably add that words are only a pale reflection of the real thing (4267).

The experience of being in a different dimension is similarly difficult to describe. The dimensions of length, breadth and depth are quite inadequate, as are time and space, to say what the dimension experienced is. The writers therefore have to circumscribe what happened and where they were by saying that they felt themselves to be somewhere else (1133), that the mind had changed gear (1239), they were put in touch with a reality beyond anything (4182) or, indeed, lifted to a different dimension (4103).

Transiency

A characteristic of many transcendent experiences is that they last for only a moment. They cannot be sustained. Even a mystical state that was sought is normally over in a flash.

Some people say that the experience lasted some minutes, but more common is the experience of one writer, who, when she 'came to', saw that the man she had been watching weighing Brussels sprouts before the experience was still doing so (2476).

One generally accepted notion of time is that it is linear: everything has a beginning in time and moves through time to an eternity. The experiences seem to show a different concept of time, which cannot be measured by a clock. Time seems not a span, but a perception, something that has no beginning or end and therefore enfolds everything and all time.

The idea of oneness that many experiences relate also includes time. It seemed to the experient that time stood still (1133; 4415), that it was outside of time (4267), that it was like hundreds of years (2476).

Intensity of the experience

Particularly in mystical experiences the content is often of a 'feeling', such as love or joy, or happiness. But what is different to this simply being a sentiment is the intensity with which love or joy or happiness is present (2461; 2726). Nothing like this has been known to the experient before. Because of this intensity, the person knows beyond doubt the reality of that feeling and of the experience.

The experience remains

Among the accounts are some written by 80- and 90-year-old people. They write about an experience they had when they were in their teens and even add that it is as fresh in their memory now as if it had just happened (2495; 4761). Other people, too, mention that the experience they had remains and does not fade with time (657; 7136).

Disappointment with help

Because the experience was so unusual, people sought help with coming to terms with it. They visited ministers and doctors, but several reported that neither Church nor medicine was helpful (2674). They were misunderstood even there where they thought religious experiences were what 'it' was about.

When do religious experiences occur?

If the experiences cannot be induced and cannot be repeated, it may be asked if there is an optimum time or precondition for them to happen. In reading the accounts it seems that there are two such instances.

Most experiences take place when the person is alone (e.g. 322; 3401; 4092). There are notable exceptions to this (2026; 3015; 4278), but they are in the minority. This seems to enhance the element of mystery and of being given something personal and unique. Perhaps alone a person is more receptive to experiences of other dimensions?

It is also remarkable how many experiences are recounted as having taken place in childhood, even early childhood (630; 2072; 2495; 4555; 4761).[20] Even though the experience may be had by a child, the essence of it is not childish (4560) and to be discarded when growing up; it stays with the person (4405), directing him or her throughout life.

The fourth characteristics of transcendent experiences noted by James, passivity, may be described here.

Although some people strive and pray for a state of mystical union, the actual experience of it cannot be worked for or brought about (2565; 4548). It can only be given. Similarly, a change, the proof of God's existence, or healing can be sought, but not induced. A transcendent experience literally comes 'out of the blue'. It is given. In that sense the recipient can 'only' receive it: he or she is a passive beneficiary. Only one person writes that he can repeat the experience, but, significantly, cannot teach his method to others (874). When an experience is induced by drugs, it is of a different quality: inferior and glossy (2366).

Most people receive such an experience gladly, but a number write that they were frightened (2596; 4232) or even terrified (4182; 4350).

Fear is a very well-known aspect of experiences recounted in the Bible. At the Annunciation, when an angel appeared to Mary to tell her that she would become the mother of Jesus, Mary was 'deeply disturbed', and the angel had to reassure her: 'Do not be afraid.'[21]

The gospels are full of references to fear on seeing Jesus in various locations.[22] It may be argued therefore that fear is a natural reaction to unusual occurrences.

Who are the experients?

Because we are situated in time and space, we experience the world around us in these dimensions. Any experience, be this a loving embrace or an accident, can be explained to other people only in terms of time and space. Therefore when we have an experience of a different dimension, we still need to explain it in these dimensions. Because it is so different, we need even more to try to make sense of it and explain it or elucidate its meaning for our life. It therefore has to be set within a framework of known facts, even if the experience itself may be left essentially unexplained.

All the writers give some information as to where they were at the time of the experience. Many give quite minute details (657; 947; 4057). Because such an experience always happens unexpectedly, many people describe what they were occupied with (2497) or thinking about (4755).

Some people also describe the cultural and religious backgrounds (2552) from which they come, so that that together with the experience forms a 'story'.

Unlike the 'visionary' experiences, which invariably mention a perceived need or difficulty, this element is not particularly obvious in 'mystical' experiences. Although some make reference to personal difficulties (2552; 2565; 4230), many particularly state that the experient was happy (657; 2476) and healthy (2366) at the time.

After this brief survey of the widely shared elements, we can now look in more detail at the experiences themselves, which we have grouped as mystical, unclassified, evil, and visionary.

Mystical Experiences

According to Parrinder, union is basic to the idea of mysticism.[23] Mystical experiences therefore are characterized by union or a sense of union. What this means is difficult to describe precisely. Many of the writers of the accounts speak of union, unity or oneness (e.g. 1239; 2848; 4230). Characteristically, with this union goes a loss of self (4664). The person becomes one with all things, and the ego is 'melted' away for the time of the experience.

The terms 'mysticism' and 'mystical' are fraught with difficulties of interpretation. The word 'mystical' as it is often used today has something dismissive about it. A person who is a dreamer, not very logical, his feet not firmly on the ground, sentimental or speaking a language in which symbols are reality can easily be labelled a 'mystic'. The mystic in religious history, however, is someone associated with contemplation. This is the person who is in touch with God and with other realities. And because these dimensions cannot be expressed easily, such a person speaks in poetic form. Words such as unity, light, opposites, marriage, revelation, being, are music to their ears and nourishment to their souls. They strive to attain a state of unity with God, with all things or with life. They strive for a *state* of unity. But an *experience* of unity – a 'religious' or 'transcendent' experience – is not necessarily a consequence. One account does show this unity after prayer (2476).

Since the accounts were written by people who were not – or did not claim to be – experts in mysticism or the language of mysticism, we are not attempting any interpretation here either. (Readers interested in the subject are referred to the Further Reading list for more information.) The writers of the accounts tell of an *experience*, and that is the point and purpose of writing them, and of reproducing them here.

A religious or transcendent experience of unity, in particular a mystical experience, is not, as the accounts show, conditional on being a mystic. Such experiences happen anywhere, at any time and to anyone. Thoughts of unity, or God, could not have been further away from some people's minds (2720; 4217; 4230).

Triggers

From the background information given by writers, it is possible to detect certain elements that seem to have triggered the experience. It is not possible to say that a view or a plant is that which brought about the experience, but the person is conscious of having noticed the view or the plant, and that the experience took place immediately afterwards.

As a very general statement, it may be said that, as mystical experiences are 'internal' and intrinsic to the person, the triggers tend to be 'external' and extrinsic to the experient.

NATURE

The majority of the mystical experiences take place in nature or out of doors (e.g. 322; 1284; 2366; 2505; 3144; 4233; etc.) or are associated with natural things, such as plants (e.g. 1136; 4230; 4384).

The 'trigger', or that which the person was aware of when the experience happened, may be looking at or being in the garden (3062; 3144; 4232), being in a field (2848), near the coast (1133; 1239; 3401; 4233), on a country lane (4103; 4415), in a meadow (4521) or even digging potatoes (2461). The person was aware of it being a fine day (1133), that the stars were visible (1136), that there was a great natural beauty (904), that the fruit on the bramble bush was glistening (2848), or that the spider plant on the windowsill was particularly beautiful (4138). Yet the experient was not physically in relation with any of these entities.

By contrast, Robinson recounts a story told by two teenagers in Canada in which the experience was not only triggered by trees, but was in and with the trees.

> We'd say 'Oh, the trees are so beautiful.' . . . But this was different. . . . then we came across this stand of birches . . . We just stood there looking at it. . . . And then – I don't know who started this – we just started laughing and hugging the birch trees. . . . This was far more than birch trees. . . . It's a feeling like you're filled up with something good.[24]

Two experiences similar in some respects are described in accounts 2505 and 4103.

PRAYER

In the archives are several accounts by people who write of having had religious experiences while praying. They do not state in more detail if they had sought such a unitive state or if the people concerned could be described as 'mystics'. All that can be said is that the experience took place while the person prayed (2526; 2565). One account (2476) is of the person engaging in prayer and devotion before the sacrament in church.

MUSIC

Many religions have esoteric practices to induce states of trance and altered consciousness. These are regarded as necessary before being initiated into certain classes of membership or leadership. Typically, such states are brought about with music, by dancing (the Whirling Dervishes), by other repeated actions such as drumming, or by eating particular foods that are said to be hallucinogenic.

It is not surprising that some of the accounts in the AHRC collection reflect such practices. Particular reference to music as being the trigger occurs several times (3670; 4548; 4693).

HEIGHTENED AWARENESS

Several accounts speak of the experient being in a state of heightened awareness before the experience itself took place (874; 947; 3062; 3144; 4071). A train of thought improved in quality (947), colours became vibrant (3062), the senses were sharpened (874). It is then difficult to distinguish between what might be described as *this* reality and *that* reality. The two may become fused, but the person remains in complete control of what is going on around him or her (947).

The content

The content, significance and particularity of mystical experiences is that sense or feeling of oneness, or unity.

James writes that:

Although so similar to states of feeling, mystical states seem to those who experience them to be also states of knowledge. They are states of insight into depths of truth unplumbed by the discursive intellect. They are illuminations, revelations, full of significance and importance.[25]

Always allowing for the difficulty of expressing adequately in words what took place, it seems nevertheless that the writers used three different ways to describe these states of unity, or oneness. The majority mentioned *union*, some talked of *being* and some mentioned *knowledge*.

UNION

The writers have described this in many different ways, each according to his or her own experience and relevance. One person calls it a unity (4384); another, a oneness with something outside of self and within (2848); a oneness of the cosmos (2461); an at-one-ment (1239).

One person felt herself to be part of nature and nature to be part of her (2668); and another, that she was in perfect harmony with every living being (3062).

Three accounts (3401; 4138; 4267) are similar in type, in that they all involve a house-plant, each being instrumental in giving the experient a sense of unity or oneness with a wider world.

BEING

It is remarkable how often that word recurs in the accounts. The person feels being part of something bigger during the experience (1133); being at one with the birds, the sea, the grass, the sky (1239); being at one with all creatures, and even the waterfalls (4233); being the fish, the music, the trees, the road (1284); being a leaf on a tree (2035). One person felt confronted with the source of all being (2848).

Two people use the phrase 'I am' to elaborate what they mean (1284; 4182). This is the phrase used by Christ on several occasions[26] and it is related to the name Yahweh (I am who I am; see p.11). The sense of being seems therefore a very powerful sense, allied to all that is, and to the ultimate Being.

KNOWLEDGE

It is probable that this is included in the state of union or being. Nevertheless, a number of writers make specific reference to it. One person writes of knowing what it was all about (322); another, tapping a universal source of knowledge (947). One writer puts it very clearly: she stepped from agnosticism to gnosis (4415).

FEELINGS

Almost all the experients describe a feeling: something experienced that is not just a sentiment and not just an outcome. These feelings are part of the actual experience. As the writers have difficulty in describing what happened, so it is difficult to be precise here what is meant by these expressions. We hope that the accounts and the writers themselves will convey what they meant.

The feeling most often experienced is love. It is not just sentimental love as it is used in everyday language; it is an overwhelming love (2565), an intense and powerful love (3191), a total love (4182).

The feeling of joy is often also experienced in superlatives: overwhelming (2720), burning (3088), even unbearable (2476).

Many other feelings are experienced, in particular peace (1239; 4230), well-being (2676), happiness (1239; 2476), serenity (4217).

One or two people describe a feeling of awe (4465) or a sensation of being holy (4340).

A somewhat different type of feeling – perhaps more a state? – is described by some writers: a sensation of being filled up (4465; 4521); an expansion is described by some others (904; 2461). This seems more a physical state than an inner feeling, though it may be difficult to describe this in terms of physiology.

Unclassified Experiences

There are certain accounts in the archives that do not at first sight fit into the two large categories (mystical and visionary), but that should not be excluded for that reason. These are in particular the psychic, out-of-body and near-death experiences. These subjects have been well researched (see Further Reading list) and accounts of such experiences were not particularly sought by the AHRC. But they arrived, and presumably with a purpose: people saw them as having 'religious' content or meaning, otherwise they would have sent them to the addresses where such accounts are specifically collected and researched.

It is not always easy to make a distinction between an out-of-body and a near-death experience. They can be quite similar. But some points can be highlighted.

- Near-death experiences seem related to severe illness (4555) or difficult labour and birth (2733).
- Out-of-body experiences do not seem to be related to illness, but happen at any time. One of the accounts states that the experience took place during prayer (2611), and another one during a dream (4496).
- In out-of-body experiences there is a dissociation with the self (the body).
- In near-death experiences the person does not seem conscious of the body, but still conscious of life and able to make rational decisions (4555).

In the accounts of near-death experiences collected by Moody,[27] many subjects describe a sensation of floating on or near the ceiling and looking down on their bodies on the bed. None of the near-death accounts used here relate this phenomenon, but one out-of-body experience does (2611).

An aspect of some of the out-of-body experiences is the experience of leaving the body through the top of the head (4496; 4764). *The Tibetan Book of the Dead*[28] has a reference to death ceremonies in which the top of the head is examined to determine if the spirit has departed from the deceased.

A graphic description of a levitation is included in the accounts (398). This is remarkable in that it happened to a child.

A number of people write about dreams (630; 2604; 4103) and indeed one of these is about an out-of-body experience (4496). Dreams have played important roles in all the ancient religions. In our own time Jung has recognized the importance of dreams in psychotherapy, for a better understanding of unconscious and conscious feeling and behaviour.[29] The dreams related here are not *about* any particular subject, but they were relevant to the person at that moment and significant enough to remember and write about.

There are two accounts that describe how the experient went through a time of 'hell' (4110; 4422). This is not the same as the pointless torment of some of the experiences of evil. Here it seems to be a 'testing by fire', lasting many hours. One person writes that only years later could she make sense of that experience by meditating on it.

As there are a number of accounts of a psychotic nature in the archives, we have included one here to represent that group (4744).

Experiences of Evil

In the archives of the AHRC are only a small number of experiences of evil. It may be that this represents an idiosyncrasy in that the requests and questionnaires did not ask for this type of experience. It may be that not many people do experience evil.

There are no particular reasons given why these experiences should occur. It seems remarkable, however, that some of them happen either to religious people (248; 4711) or in religious places (3191).

The characteristic of all these experiences is the utter sense of fear, terror and horror that they induce (248; 4325).

It may be simply coincidence, but it is worth noting, that while many of the 'ordinary' experiences may last for a very short time, some of the experients describe these experiences as lasting for a long time (3191) or even a whole night (4325).

Visionary Experiences

In contrast to the mystical experiences, where very often one can detect a sense of 'absence' – a loss of self – the visionary experiences have an element of 'presence' – something (or someone) else is present with the person.

These visionary experiences are clearly in the majority of the accounts in the archives. But first of all, a word of explanation for the name of these experiences.

It has been said that seeing is the most important sense for a person. Hearing comes next in importance, and touch, smell and taste follow in descending order of importance. There may be some truth in this, which may be reflected in the fact that there are so many experiences where something is seen, fewer where something is heard, a number where something is perceived through touch, only one where smell is involved (2674) and none at all where taste is described. Nevertheless we are grouping these all under the general title of 'visionary' simply for the sake of convenience and accessibility.

Within this broad category the presences fall into two kinds: the presence of a light or lights, and the presence of a figure, such as Jesus, an angel or saint, or the dead. These are again only very broad categories. Within them there are many variations and overlap frequently occurs. Some experiences could be described as part mystical and part visionary.

One striking difference between visionary and mystical experiences is that here the writers seem not to have the same difficulty of putting into words what happened to them. They are dealing more with the known than the unknown, even though what they see are not everyday occurrences. They are dealing with something almost tangible, and therefore words are more easily available.

Just as some mystical experiences describe an intensity of feelings, so some of the writers of the visionary experiences say how strong the experience itself was (4232). In particular, three writers felt that it pervaded their whole bodies so that they felt they had to 'hold on' for fear that they were too fragile to contain the experience (3088; 4581; 4713).

Experiences of light

The experiences in which the writers describe seeing a light are very diverse in character.

Some of the accounts could be called mystical in that they have elements of oneness (2062; 2476; 4230; 4548). But mystical experiences rarely occur when the person is in a state of stress or distress. Yet about half of the accounts that relate seeing a light start by saying that the writer was in some kind of physical or mental distress (1136; 2010; 2026; 2479; 2524; 4057; 4230; 4545).

A number of the experiences of seeing a light take place either in nature (4405) or connected with nature in that the light seemed to be triggered by a star (1136) or by looking out of the window (4230), or the light filled the house and garden (4267).

Some writers describe the light by its colour: golden (2479; 4267; 4384), white (322; 4136; 4545) or blue (3670; 4057). Some people put the light into recognizable form and size, such as a dinner plate (4545). One person described it as filling her body (4103) and one saw the light moving (4545).

Some accounts of seeing a light speak of it as a power (2479), a pulsing dynamo (4267) or a field of energy (1143).

For some people the light seemed to be a prelude to an experience of the presence of a figure (2720), the Holy Trinity (4230) or a firm hand on the shoulder (2524).

One person experienced this light in a dream (4103).

The experiences where a figure or presence is seen invariably end with the writer saying that she or he was comforted, healed or otherwise restored. These writers – like those who have had mystical experiences – speak more often of a state of peace (2479; 4230) or of a knowledge gained (4548).

Experiences of a voice

Hearing a voice is in most experiences related to seeing a presence, be this a light or a sacred figure. The voice is therefore an integral part of the vision.

But there are some accounts (143; 1145; 4114) that mention only hearing a voice; they do not mention any other feature present.

The messages are short, direct and totally relevant to the experient. (See also p.35.)

Experiences of touch

There are a number of experiences where the person describes being touched. As with voices, this happens mainly in the context of a wider vision, but some accounts mention only the touch, and this is the experience (640; 2524). In all cases this is a benevolent touch and one that the person seems happy to experience.

Experiences of a presence

The experiences of a presence form the larger part of the accounts in the archives of the AHRC. The fact that these were, and are often called, 'religious experiences' may be misleading people into thinking that such experiences are about God, or holy or religious presences. There are indeed many accounts that speak of the presence of God, but other presences, such as angels, saints or unnamed figures, are also frequent. And last, but not least, many people have written of experiences of the presence of someone who has died.

Triggers

As with the mystical experiences, it is possible in this type, too, to note certain triggers. But with this being such a different experience, it is not surprising that the triggers to visionary experiences are also very different from the mystical types.

We described the mystical experiences as 'internal' and their triggers as 'external'. By contrast, the visionary experiences are 'external': something outside of the person is seen, heard or perceived. The trigger appears to be something internal, inside the person. It is not possible to say that that internal factor *actually* started the experience, but the person was clearly aware of a state or condition before the experience happened. This seems to be almost without exception a state of trouble, anguish or stress. Many people describe in detail mental anguish (630; 2563), stress (2049; 3015), depression (2565; 4410), nervous breakdown (446; 4114; 4521) and going through an ordeal (2524). Very often this stress or trouble is related to the death of a close or dear person (e.g., 2674; 4104; 4365; 4496; 2604).

The descriptions of the state of mind and soul seem almost in an effort to explain the experience. What is quite evident, too, is that that state is not simply a 'bad day', but a desperate situation, when seemingly nothing short of a miracle could help or extricate the person from the predicament.

PRAYER

A number of experients write that they prayed for help or release, change or healing (e.g., 639; 640; 1145; 2562; 2657), or quasi-prayed (4545). The greater majority do not write of any explicit prayer or request. But many people write of their experiences as an answer to prayer (e.g., 639; 2562), some being emphatic that someone need only pray to be helped (2009).

THE NEED FOR HEALING

Some of the accounts refer to physical illness and pain, some of it having lasted a long time or having been debilitating (639; 2657; 4426).

The greater number of experients write about mental, psychological and spiritual anguish and trouble (e.g., 446; 2565; 4114). While suffering of the body is real and limiting, suffering of the mind is literally soul-destroying.

THE NEED FOR CHANGE

This is more difficult to define, but the need for a change of mind (248), the need to make sense of existence (640) and an awareness of being self-conscious and uncertain (2526) are mentioned.

Some people write of difficult relationships, and that their experiences helped them to see how to proceed (3670).

THE NEED FOR HELP

This is a general title to cover various types of need: to be allowed to live (630), while going through an ordeal (2524), to cope while a son is ill far away (2563), while the person is in prison (2723), while having personal difficulties (4768).

THE NEED FOR SAFETY

There are numbers of accounts in the archives where precognition alerts people to danger (4063 is an example). They are remarkable in that the safety need is for others, not for oneself.

Safety on a dark road is experienced differently by one person (2602).

THE NEED FOR PROOF

A number of experients write that they were looking for proof that God exists (2530; 3009; 4465). Their accounts give details of an almost desperate search.

THE NEED FOR COMFORT

This need is stated almost exclusively by people who have been bereaved and are grieving deeply (e.g., 2010: 2497; 4281; 4365) and by a person caring for a dying relative (2026).

PATTERNING

Because many of the experients put their accounts on to a backcloth of happenings in everyday life, they can see patterns emerge. The patterns may not be evident at first, but as the people become aware of events, they see them linking up (414; 1145; 1637; 4540; 4629) and become aware of being guided (4248). As this is possible only with hindsight, it is all the more remarkable that the experience had such a central place in a person's life that many events and situations can be referred to it.

In the accounts there is only one of the person himself as he should be in the *future* (4107). Perhaps that capacity of seeing into the future normally exists for and about other people and things, rather than about oneself?

A somewhat different type of patterning could be described as synchronicity. Here, an event takes place in one location and another person is aware of it (1145; 2547; 4063). It seems more than simple telepathy, because in some accounts there is intense suffering present for both parties (4232).

The content

The distinctive element in visionary experiences is a presence. It is mostly seen and heard, or felt and heard. Three types of presence can be distinguished.

THE PRESENCE OF GOD

The word 'God' represents someone or something to the majority of people. Most of the accounts were written by people living in the British Isles or elsewhere within a context where Christianity is the traditional religion. God is therefore taken to be the God of the Bible, and the person who has an experience of God is familiar – at least to some extent – with forms and terms of faith, and private and public prayer and worship.

A small study of religious experiences in India showed that 'the Hindu respondents have referred to different manifestations of Him, such as Venketeshwara Bhairava (the deity of the healing professions), Krishna, Kali, besides, of course, The God Almighty.'[30]

Some experients have difficulty in writing about God. They are

not entirely happy to call him 'God' (947; 2848; 4278) or they are
not sure who or what God is (630; 4092).

Characteristics of an experience of God are that the person has
no doubt that it is God – whatever she or he calls him. It may be
God the Father (4761) or Jesus (4713), Christ (2720; 4465), the
Lord (2596; 4327; 4332), the Saviour (657), the Holy Spirit (2497)
or the Holy Trinity (4230).

In other experiences only some aspect of God is felt: the hand of
God (4384), the hem of his garment (2498).

Thirdly, only a feeling is present, like being hugged by God
(4365), but not a complete presence.

In some of the accounts of the presence of God mention is made
of a power present that is more difficult to describe (640; 3191;
4092). Some experients also refer to the God within (4440; 4581).

A SACRED PRESENCE NOT CALLED GOD

This is a real or quasi-real presence and a recognizable form, seen,
heard and felt, of a figure that the person either recognizes or
knows about.

Some accounts are hesitant to give any name or definition to this
presence. They speak of a masculine presence (2074; 2643), a lady
(4545), someone (446) or simply a presence (4113). Yet others are
aware of only some aspect of a presence, such as a wing (4067).
Besides that, there are accounts of a non-physical presence, where
the experient simply knew or felt but in a way different from the
ordinary (3020; 4560). Whatever the presence, it was instinctively
experienced as good (4560) and benign.

A curious but noteworthy phenomenon of some of these experiences is that the 'person' seen is taller than life-size (2074; 2676;
3144). No particular reason is given by the experients. Tales and
legends are peppered with giants and since religious experiences
are linked with the collective unconscious and psychic forces,
perhaps any explanations for this occurrence should be sought in
that realm.

The variety of these presences is surprising. History would lead
one to believe that the most common of these presences would be
angels and saints, yet only one account mentions a guardian angel
(3020) and one an archangel (4067).

THE PRESENCE OF THE DEAD

The Christian tradition has, on the whole, been sceptical about experiences of the presence of the dead, relegating them to spiritualism and primitive cults. But the fact is that there are a great many accounts that relate experiences of meeting with someone who has died. The way in which the accounts are written shows also that the experients did not feel that this was a purely psychic experience. Meeting with that particular person was a religious experience, something that points beyond itself.

The dead person is always very clearly recognized. It is not simply a person, but 'my husband' (4104), 'my grandmother' (2563; 3020).

The experiences of the presence of the dead tend to occur more frequently in the days and weeks after the death of the person (2497; 4104; 4281; 4365) and only occasionally some years later (2563; 2604).

The dead person is usually seen, sometimes heard, and rarely felt (1131).

In our culture, where the presence of the dead is mostly portrayed in the form of ghosts and caricatured as 'things that go bump in the night', the experiences recounted here are remarkably gentle, comforting and even joyful.

HEARING VOICES

Several accounts mention that the experient had heard a voice or received a message (e.g., 143; 4410). A few writers attribute the voice to God (3670; 4327; 4711; 4761). Most of them speak simply of a voice, though from the context of the account it could be deduced that it might have been God. Very rarely are visions of the dead accompanied by a voice (3020), or even a conversation (2547).

Some accounts make a clear distinction between a voice heard *within* (4114), and a voice heard *without* (4350), i.e., an audible voice distinct from the person, perceived with the physical ears. Most writers simply say that they heard a voice, without specifying how or where it came from. Some of the writers of these accounts were astonished to hear God, or any voice at all, and one thought

that it was one of her children calling (2498). This is reminiscent
of the biblical story of Samuel, who also didn't recognize the voice
of God, but thought it was his teacher, Eli.[31]

The message that this voice gives is generally short, direct and
completely understandable by the experient (143; 1136), even
though to an outsider or reader it may not appear obvious or
intelligent at all. Although the words are clear, their meaning may
not be (4711) (see p.12) or may become clear only later.

Outcomes of the Experiences

Most of the accounts of transcendent experiences follow the pattern
of a beginning, a middle and an end. The beginning is the
background and context, the middle is the description of the
experience and the end is the outcome, or what the person
perceives to be different afterwards.

As each experience is clearly adapted to the needs, circumstances
and knowledge of the person who receives it, so the outcomes are
also very individual. Nevertheless, it is possible to describe some
types of outcomes which are frequently reported. Outcomes of
experiences of evil, however, do not fit these patterns, and we are
unable to generalize about them.

> immediately practical;
> healing;
> change;
> good feelings.

Immediately practical outcomes

These are often related to visionary experiences. The person who
was in need of help got it (2479); the person in prison and crying
to God was reassured (2723); the person who needed the rain to
stop saw it come about (3009); the writer who, after an experience,
cooked an inspired supper (4278); the bereaved person who was
able to control her emotion (2010); the husband in danger was
rescued in time (4063); and the woman who was afraid on a dark
road had a companion walk with her (2602).

Healing

Many of the accounts of healing are quite dramatic. There was no more mental trouble (446); a leg got better immediately (2562; 4426); a person at a low ebb felt peaceful (4230). These experients write of complete healing, while others state that they still have trouble but can now cope (2524; 2657; 4230; 4267; 4768).

Change

It is not easy to describe change. Many of the writers state how they changed in their relationships with other people. They are more tolerant of others (874), have more empathy (4764), are more humble (583; 4465), more sensitive to the needs of others (2526).

One person writes that she is aware that life has changed, but is unable to describe how (4127), and another has noticed that her body is changing (2547). One says that she is no longer shy (4540); two that they had a permanent smile (1136; 2720).

There are several accounts that describe a conversion (e.g., 248, 2011, 3088, 4091, 4340, 4713), whether or not that word is used. A conversion is a complete turning and change by the person. The experience of it is dramatic, not only for the person concerned, but also for those around (4340).

A small number of people make reference to things that they felt called to because of the experience. A commitment in prayer (4768) and prayer for others (4711) are the clearest statements.

Comfort

Some of the individuals who write of deep distress after the death of a loved one also write particularly of being comforted after the experience (2010; 2604; 2674).

Certainty

The characteristic of James's elements of mystical experiences that has not yet been dealt with is the noetic quality – a knowledge that

the experient gains, which is of a very particular kind.[32] It is a
certainty that is quite unshakeable (4496; 4581). There is a sense
in which the person is not to worry any more (2062); doubt is
dispelled (3088); everything makes sense (4092); there is 'something there' (4560).

This knowledge can perhaps best be summed up under three
headings:

'All will be well'

This saying is like a refrain through the accounts (4404; 4548;
4614). Its author, Julian of Norwich (see p.12), is not one of the
better-known writers – she is not even a canonized saint.

The certainty for the experients seems to be not only 'all is well',
but, indeed, 'all *shall* be well, and all shall be well, and all manner
of thing shall be well.'[33]

Faith is strengthened

It may at first seem logical that those who had a visionary experience
or an encounter with God should have their faith in him confirmed
or strengthened. But people who had mystical experiences also
write that faith in God was the result (3020; 4185). Those who had
faith already now find it to be like a rock (4340; 4405). There is
now a conviction of the reality of God (4092; 4384).

Towards the end of his life the psychologist C. J. Jung apparently
said that he did not believe any more that God existed; he *knew* he
did. This sounds contradictory in terms, but it seems to be also the
experience of some of the writers of these accounts (4232; 4248;
4405; 4465).

No fear of death

It is most often the people who had a near-death experience (2733;
2596; 2674) or who have had an experience of the dead who then
claim that the fear of death disappears (2676; 3020). But people
who had mystical experiences are left with the same conclusion.

Good feelings

It seems almost logical that a good experience leaves a person with
good feelings, but what the writers describe is far from sentimental.

Many experience a love (e.g., 2049; 4340) that goes beyond the self (3062) and that is not self-interested or self-directed.

Other people experience joy (2476; 2720; 4113). This is more than gladness; it is an intense joy (2726), not just a feeling, but a reality (2552; 4607; 4185; 4422).

A sometimes unexpected outcome is a sense of peace. This peace is not something temporary; it is simply a fact of life from that point on (e.g., 874; 2049; 2479; 2495; 3006; 4185; 4230; 4404). It is a state that stays with the person always, and which he or she can recall and use in times of stress (2026). It seems that particularly during illness or at or before an operation (4138) this peace can give assurance and remove fear.

The Purpose of a Religious or Transcendent Experience

Some of the writers of accounts have added their interpretations of the experiences they had. Many see in the outcome the purpose of the experience itself.

On reading through the accounts it seems that the purpose of a religious experience is to reveal something that ordinary consciousness and this dimension are not able to reveal, or at least not easily, for whatever reasons. The experience seems to want to reach out to, or give, something bigger, greater, more complete than what is there at present. This generally seems to be for the sake of others or for the common good.

Any transcendent experience has the possibility to alter a person's values (2476). Values can become hardened or outdated, and a change may come about only with a jolt.

One person has found that the experiences helped her to think more deeply about the 'otherness' of natural things, and to evolve some sort of philosophy to try to sort out the mysteries of 'being' and 'not being' (4693).

Another person writes that the ethics of her creed are enough for daily living. When these degenerate or break down and no friends are available to come to the rescue, the help she receives from above restores the equilibrium (143). Others write similarly.

Whatever 'it' is is there to help and direct in ways that would not
be available otherwise (2552; 4110).

The experiences are not only answers and rescuers, they add
depth and an extra dimension to life that would not have been
there before (4465).

Life is one long process of change and adaptation. Hay writes
that

in terms of their capacity to adjust to their personal situation, those
claiming religious experience state that it has aided them to behave more
competently than before. They are, on average, happier and more optimis-
tic about life than other people.[34]

Not only does a religious experience call for change, but it seems
to enable change, and to do this by equipping the person with the
necessary mental stamina, in one case someone who was suffering
acute mental illness at the time (446).

What is the Meaning of a Religious or a Transcendent Experience?

Clearly many people would like, and need, help with their religious
experiences. They need to understand the experience itself and
what it means to them (4755). Indeed, how are they to know that
their experiences are valid, and not a delusion, or caused by illness,
drugs or magic influences? How are they to know that their
interpretation of it is right? They may be like St Francis going off
doing something as a result of such an experience, only to find out
later that they had misunderstood the meaning (see p.12).

It is beyond the scope of this book to go into details on this
aspect, and the reader is referred to the Further Reading list for
more information. However, in this last part of the descriptions of
religious experiences we, the editors, are allowing ourselves to
make some general interpretations regarding the meaning of these
experiences.

The most striking element of the religious and other transcendent experiences in the collection at the AHRC is their constant
affirmation of life. They are enhancing and enriching life; they
point forward; they are positive; they are benign.

They are also, to coin a phrase, 'people friendly'. They are geared to the individual, his or her needs, conscious or unconscious, perceived or implied.

Therefore, one criterion for assessing the authenticity of such an experience seems to be *if it enhances life and leaves the person 'better' or more whole, and that person then uses the experience in the service of others*.

Various people have attempted to describe what this life-enhancing element is. It has been called 'dropping the mask' or 'persona'[35] or, as Maslow put it, someone who has had peak experiences has 'become more a *real* person'.[36] There is no need any more to hide anything. The oneness either experienced or given does away with the need to show only one part of the person to the world.

This may also be of some help to those who help others with their experiences, be these in psychotherapy, spiritual direction, counselling or in psychiatric institutions. If the experience points beyond itself, and beyond the self, then it is almost certainly to be relied on.

An experience is not magic. People who have had experiences still struggle; they still have pain and suffering. An experience is enhancing. Julian of Norwich wrote after her experiences, 'He did not say, "You shall not be tempest-tossed, you shall not be work-weary, you shall not be discomforted." But he said, "You shall not be overcome." '[37]

An experience that is true will be true thoughout life. Its character is personal and also universal. It is practical and also symbolic. This is clearly evident throughout history. The call to St Francis of Assisi has led to a world-wide movement. The experience on the road to Damascus led St Paul to preach Christianity in undreamt-of places and situations. The experiences of the Buddha under the bo-tree have been relevant to millions of people over thousands of years and are gaining rather than losing relevance today. An experience seems to be in 'one man' but for 'Everyman'.

The design and meaning of a religious experience seem not so much to lie in an outcome or a measurable goal, but in keeping to the original vision, remaining faithful or – as in the Judaeo-Christian language – 'remembering' and in this strength constantly enhancing life.

Maslow states that experients become 'more spontaneous and

honest and innocent'.[38] This last seems to compare with the saying 'Unless you change and become like little children you will never enter the kingdom of heaven.'[39] It is almost as if through education and the need to be somebody or something, we have lost a wholeness that belongs only to 'children' – the innocents. Change is one of the needs frequently mentioned in the accounts. Perhaps the unknown or unconscious need for change is to become like a child again so as to be able to take part in life fully.

Somewhat connected with this is the often quoted assertion that after an experience the person is not afraid of death any more. Death is the great unknown, particularly in this day and age. When most people will never have seen someone die, let alone a dead body, the fear of death – and the annihilation it brings – can be very strong. The religious language of earlier centuries – of eternal life, of visions of heaven and assurance of sins forgiven – is not nearly as current and relevant today. A religious experience, therefore, may be not only a gift, but a necessary form of establishing an equilibrium in the understanding of life in general and individual life in particular.

In and through a transcendent experience a person becomes more and more aware, and – given the right conditions – more responsible, active and capable of fulfilling the creative potential. This makes a person more free. She or he is more able to know, choose and act on the values that are relevant. Some accounts have expressed this as 'thy will be done' (4071; 4248; 4465). This does not seem to be an abdication of will, but a going along with the life-force – that which is greater – rather than grabbing at something small and of little value.

In our heart of hearts each one of us knows that life is a mystery – where did we come from, where are we going, what is our purpose, and more profoundly still, what sort of creatures are we, spiritually and physically intermingled as we are? We know a great deal about the physical world of which we are a part, and which itself is miraculous and wonderfully constructed, but the glimpses of the other non-physical, spiritual world experienced by the writers of the accounts remind us that there is another reality in which we also seem to participate. They show us that 'religious' experiences are not just things of the past, enshrined in Holy Writ or occurring only to saints, but that they happen to a great many ordinary people today. They seem to affirm the immanence of the spiritual reality within the physical reality.

Frankl points out that human beings do not *create* the meaning in their lives, but they *discover* it.[40] This seems to be one of the most urgent tasks of our day. A transcendent experience may be a vehicle for this discovery. But such an experience cannot be wished or conjured into being. It happens when the conditions are right. It seems that as more and more people are claiming to have had one or several experiences, this is actually helping individuals and the collective consciousness to find meaning in life on a personal and global level.

What about the people who have not had a religious or transcendent experience? Or those who have had them without acknowledging them or taking them seriously?

We do not yet know why some people have experiences and others don't. Part of the mystery of the transcendent is precisely in its 'illogical' appearance and its transiency, and in the fact that it can only be received, not worked for.

The writer of the following letter must represent many people. There is a longing and a knowledge that such experiences could have 'endless uses'. Perhaps it is not only the experiences that count but an openness to all things in and around us, in particular to that 'power from beyond ourselves' that 'is in our souls all the time' and helps us indeed to see the invisible.

F. ?(?)   4653

I have pondered a few years now over the subject of transcendent experience and never been able to describe my feelings.

Although this wonderful feeling hasn't happened to myself, I try to understand and reach out to it. I realize that something is missing in my spiritual side and try to find this missing link. This realization of the great presence is a gift given; it cannot be bought or sought after. I slightly envy those who are settled and have an inner calmness.

Perhaps this power is in our souls all the time and it is up to ourselves to be at one with it. Basically, it could be the battle of one's will between good and evil. Subconsciously, throughout one's life this battle can go on and then, when the greater wins, consciously this is recognized, in either good terms or bad: the spiritual recognition or an evil act. Well, anyway, this is my thoughts on the subject.

But if it doesn't come from within onself, where does it come from? I try so hard to understand it. I can touch it slightly, but can't grasp it. I know, whatever it is, that it's there. I can feel somewhere in my heart that I should not have to worry for the future, because it may have its bumps but, on the whole, nothing can destroy it. Only the person who made it can destroy it. And I strongly believe that almost everyone has this hope inside them.

I know something is there, but just can't make that vital contact. Perhaps I'm rejecting it. This type of recognition could have endless uses. To bring hope and love into the lives of people who have never felt warmth in their hearts before. The criminals, mental patients and even the lonely could be helped with this wonderful gift.

SINGLE EXPERIENCES

*

A large proportion of the accounts in the archives at the AHRC are letters of people who describe only one experience in their lives. Such experiences are as varied as the people themselves in terms of when they took place, where the person was, the background and 'history' of the person, what, if anything, might have triggered it and what the content of the experience was.

We present these accounts as they stand, having attempted merely to group them loosely as to their content, following the order of description in the preceding chapter: mystical, 'unclassified', evil and visionary experiences.

Each person has written a personal story, but in publishing them some of the personal touches of the letters are lost – the handwriting, the paper used, the signature – but we hope that their content will still speak.

F. 40 (23)   322

I am enclosing a description of an unexplained incident which occurred some years ago. I have since tried to rationalize it many times (but very unsatisfactorily), mainly because the setting was too ideal and full of dramatic grandeur for a genuine spiritual experience – far rather that it had happened while I was boiling an egg! Although I have walked cliff paths with waves smashing on rocks many times since, and indeed before, with the same exhilaration, I have never enjoyed a repeat performance.

At the age of 23, my husband and I were walking a cliff path in Cornwall. It was a bright sunny day in September, bright but not a garish mid-summer sun. My husband was walking his usual forty yards ahead and disappeared over the brow of an incline, so to all intents and purposes I was entirely alone. Although there was no mist, the light seemed suddenly white and diffused and I experienced the most incredible sense of oneness and at the same time 'knew what it was all about', 'it' being existence. Of course, seconds later I hadn't the faintest idea what it was all about. However, it struck me that the oneness was in part explained by the sensation that the air and space and light was somehow tangible, one could almost grasp it, so that there wasn't a space which stopped because my human form was there, but that my form was merely a continuity of the apparently solid space.

The experience was unbelievably beautiful, and I will never forget the quality of that bright white light. It was awesome.

F. 21 (19)   1133

I have recently left art college, where I have been studying painting for five years.

Neither my father nor my mother went to church or had any religious belief. I have not been christened and was always encouraged from an early age to sort out my own feelings about religion. Any religious education I had at school I barely tolerated.

About two years ago, while on holiday in Cornwall, I went for a walk with my sister along the beach. It was a fine day, the sea, cliffs and sky were perfect. I had often seen that particular place before but on this day I felt very strange.

My sister had walked on in front of me; I was left alone. It was as if time had stood still. I could think of nothing, I only felt I was 'somewhere else'. I was part of something bigger and absolutely beyond me. My problems and my life didn't matter at all because I was such a tiny part of a great whole. I felt a tremendous relief. I was aware of my eyes not only looking at, but feeling, the beauty of everything that was there for eternity.

I don't know how long I stood there; it could have been two minutes or twenty. My sister came back, spoke to me and we walked back together.

I have never forgotten that day. Because of that experience I have become extremely interested in many different types of religions and philosophies, and have found many descriptions of experiences similar to mine.

Whether it came from a power outside or a psychological need on my part I can't tell.

F. 38 (?) 1239

I was standing alone on the edge of a low cliff overlooking a small valley leading to the sea. It was late afternoon or early evening and there were birds swooping in the sky – possibly swallows. Suddenly my mind 'felt' as though it had changed gear or twitched into another view of things. I still saw the birds and everything around me but instead of standing looking at them, I *was* them and they were me. I was also the sea and the sound of the sea and the grass and sky. Everything and I were the same, all one. It was the most peaceful and 'right' feeling imaginable and I knew without any smallest doubt that everything happened for a reason, a good reason, and fitted into everything else, like an arch with all the bricks supporting each other and their cornerstone without cement, just by their being there. I was filled, swamped, with happiness and peace. Everything was RIGHT.

I don't know how long it lasted, probably only a second or two. I have never had this again and am told that it is an early stage of

awareness of a desperate need for 'at-one-ment', to which those
who think about these things are striving.

M. 71 (47)   1284

I was sitting on a low wall on the outskirts of the town of C. Across
the road was a wayside 'tea-shop' stall with the proprietor in full
view serving two customers. The branches of two small trees next
to the stall waved in the moderately strong breeze and the sun
shone with some glare on the white, dusty road, along which came
some fishermen with baskets of fish on their heads. From the
second storey of a nearby building I could hear a nautch tune.
Then, as the fishermen came abreast of me, one fish, alive, flapped
up and seemed to stand on its tail and bow. I felt great compassion
for the fish.

Suddenly everything was transformed, transfigured, translated,
transcended. All was fused into one. I was the fish. The sun sang
and the road sang. The music shone. The hands of the stall-keeper
danced. The branches of the trees danced. All in time with the
same music. They were the music and I was the music and I was
the fish, the fishermen, the hands of the stall-keeper, the trees, the
branches, the road, the sun, the music: all one and nothing
separate. Not parts of the one but the one itself.

I was at the time 47 years old. Am male, born in a (Roman)
Catholic family. Could not accept that teaching as given. Born in a
small country town of Australia.

Effects

I am not your 'friend and brother': I am you and you are me and
'before Abraham was, I am'. I am something like Browning's
Lazarus:

> Discourse to him of prodigious armaments
> assembled to besiege his city now,
> or of the passing of a mule with gourds,
> 'tis one.

Not altogether, and not all the time. I can be concerned and, to
some extent, shaken.

M. ? (?) 2035

I was lying in a field under a tree thinking rather deeply of love and the joy it brings. Suddenly I became aware of myself as being a leaf hanging on that tree. All materialism disappeared completely, and I felt like a torch burning in the darkness. I seemed to be filled with the rays of the sun. This experience lasted for about three minutes. It is interesting to note that my behaviour pattern has changed since this experience. I feel a lot more peaceful and happier within myself, and I look upon life as being a spiritual evolution within a material body.

F. 36 (8) 2366

I would like to contribute a description of an experience which I had the summer of my (I think) eighth birthday. I am American, born in New York City. I graduated from college, have spent much of the last twelve years in Europe and have read a great deal of parapsychological literature, expecially because I have had a number of such experiences myself.

As far as I can remember, I have always believed in a Supreme Being and the immanence of that Power. My father, who had been brought up a Catholic, died in the war. Spiritual and mystical things were never mentioned in my home and I kept quite silent about what I believed and experienced. The summer after my father's death we lived at my grandmother's house by the New England coast. I spent most of the time alone exploring. There were about twenty-five acres, I suppose, but I was fascinated by detail. I had some idea I could collect patterns of natural things: crystals, twigs and leaves (and, ultimately, also snowflakes). I drew these collections clumsily and hoarded bits of objects in shoe boxes. I was well-fed and healthy. Although I do feel the heat and it was a sunny day, I am sure what happened was not caused by too much sun, too little food or too much activity. Or growing pains.

I had found several (I think) garnet crystals in some large greyish boulders, which formed the breakwater of the property where a wide pasture sloped quite steeply down to the water. I was determined to somehow chip these garnets out (I have them still today). This involved squatting in the muddy sand and chipping away with a small hammer and chisel. I wasn't very good at this and I had never found anyone to show me how to do it properly. But I spent hours at it, happily.

That one day, as I was choosing which crystal to try for, the field of my vision grew brighter, a kind of dancing brightness like heat over sand, like the quite colourless light in some parts of a candle flame. All awareness of any light source vanished: there were no shadows. There was also no weight. Or mass. Each particle spread, suspended in relation to every other, first of the rock I was facing so close, which was no longer dark grey, then of this rock in relation to the other boulders behind it, then of these to the earth, of the sloping land behind it, of the globe itself. I seemed to see in and in, deeper and clearer and further, not a pattern in a flat sense – there was nothing flat or static – but lightly (floatingly) free and deep in, brightly. I don't think I had learned much of anything yet about geology or glaciers; my interest in collecting little stones and crystals was something quite private and perhaps even (unconsciously) magical. But in that moment I seemed to see the grading of substance, the erratics dragged and mixed with the eroded sand and earth and the top soil; the whole cycle, the interpenetration and overlap of sea and earth and air. It wasn't just a grading down and grinding and coming to rest, it was a constant spiraling linking and reshaping.

I was aware while I was experiencing this that I had previously considered symmetry and symmetrical forms the most perfect and special, but now I saw others which were more important, spirals (helical? shapes) and other patterns more like waves (or waves in place, the way wind affects a wheat field), and the fact that this pattern or this reality derived its energy from asymmetry. I saw this all at once, but I can't write it down like that. I thought of stars then, not atoms: I don't think I had heard about them yet. There was a linking of these, which was very bright. When I try to think about it, I can't be sure if all of these filaments of light were linking or if some were perhaps the trails of their movements. I knew I was also held in this unity, every bit of me. I didn't look at myself (I'm not sure I moved my eyes either) but I knew I was also waves and these light lovely concentrations. I was the same as what was opening up before me (or I was opening up too).

I was still myself (I didn't *merge*) in the sense that I still saw all this from a consciousness, but it did change not only my beliefs but also my sense of bodies and material things, of interdependence, of holiness or value.

The air, too (or the spaces between what I saw moving), was not empty or passive. And the further I saw in, the brighter and more audible it grew. It wasn't just seeing into elements or earth. I knew more surely than what one can learn from books that life (and also 'inanimate' objects) are held in a unity, that one is also part of this unity, not fatalistically, not mechanistically, not rigidly in any symmetrical way either. Light was part of the unity as well as the general motion.

Even though this experience lasted perhaps a couple of minutes, it was so peaceful and joyous. I felt lighter. I have had experiences which seem to be reminders since then. Sometimes when I start thinking about this way of seeing, it is so exclusive that I find it difficult to shift focus back to everyday. I think people who have experienced similar visions and clarities tend to try to put them in familiar words and images, and these words reveal their backgrounds but perhaps aren't exactly right about the vision itself. Perhaps when part of the vision is revealing 'how things work', what comes across is 'the machine' and then people describe gears and cogwheels and hums of motors. Perhaps because I was focusing on stones and natural forms which I loved, these gave me the opening or the way I saw, because they were the way I was capable then of being reached further, because of my awe for these shapes. Otherwise, perhaps the light would have been too sudden and too intense and I wouldn't have been able to see it or to stand it. Doesn't awe, inclination or faith predetermine how much you can endure, or determine how much you have opened yourself to take in of this particular focus before it is too bright?

I may add that I once tried mescalin and have had hashish three times in the last five years. I felt these drug experiences were not the same, not only because I didn't learn anything as profound, but also because my conscious self wasn't the same in relation to what I saw, but maybe this sort of thing is a question of degree. These drug experiences seemed inferior, impermanent, working upon me; glossier.

F. ? (30)   2848

One day years ago I went for a walk in the fields with my dog.
My mind suddenly started thinking about the beauty around me,
and I considered the marvellous order and timing of the growth
of each flower, herb and the abundance of all the visible growth
going on around. I remember thinking 'Here is mind'. Then we
had to get over a stile and suddenly I was confronted with a
bramble bush which was absolutely laden with black glistening
fruit. And the impact of that, linked with my former reasoning,
gave me a great feeling of ecstasy. For a few moments I really did
feel at one with the Universe or the Creative Power we recognize.
I know it was a feeling of oneness with something outside my
self, and also within. I must have been confronted with the source
of all being, whatever one should call it. I have often told my
friends about it, though it seems too sacred to talk about. The
experience has never been forgotten. It was quite electric and
quite unsought.

F. 56 (16)   4405

I decided to write after keeping my experience to myself for forty
years. I was 16 and had always enjoyed solitary walks around my
village home. One evening I set out, by myself, as usual, to walk up
a lane towards the wood. I was not feeling particularly happy or
particularly sad, just ordinary. I was certainly not 'looking' for
anything, just going for a walk to be peaceful. It must have been
August, because the corn was ripe and I only had a summer dress
and sandals on. I was almost to the wood when I paused, turned to
look at the cornfield, took two or three steps forward so I was able
to touch the ears of corn and watched them swaying in the faint
breeze. I looked to the end of the field – it had a hedge then – and
beyond that to some tall trees towards the village. The sun was
over to my left; it was not in my eyes.

   Then . . . there must be a blank. I will never know for how long,
because I was only in my normal conscious mind with normal
faculties as I came out of it. Everywhere surrounding me was this
white, bright, sparkling light, like sun on frosty snow, like a million

diamonds, and there was no cornfield, no trees, no sky, this *light* was everywhere; my ordinary eyes were open, but I was not seeing with them. It can only have lasted a moment I think or I would have fallen over.

The feeling was indescribable, but I have never experienced anything in the years that followed that can compare with that glorious moment; it was blissful, uplifting, I felt open-mouthed wonder.

Then the tops of the trees became visible once again, then a piece of sky and gradually the *light* was no more, and the cornfield was spread before me. I stood there for a long time, trying in vain for *it* to come back and have tried many times since, but I only saw it once; but I know in my heart it is still there – and here – and everywhere around us. I know *Heaven* is within us and around us. I have had this wonderful experience which brought happiness beyond compare.

We see God in the miracle of life, in trees, flowers and birds – I smile when I hear talk of God as a man, wrathful or otherwise – I *know* I have seen and felt and am humbly grateful for the inner rock to which I cling.

I wrote it down, but I never told anybody.

F. 53 (39) 44¹5

I was walking up the country lane approaching our Welsh home. It was a beautiful May afternoon and I rejoiced in the loveliness of the familiar scene. I had said, perhaps a day or two before: 'I abandon myself to you, dark spirits.' This was no invocation of 'demons'. I meant the mysterious forces of life which lay outside my conscious control.

I was relaxed and happy as I walked.

Suddenly, everything stopped. I stopped. The birds were no longer singing. The distant traffic sounds from the village ceased. Nothing moved. Utter silence, utter stillness. The May sunlight was transformed into a white radiance.

I don't know how long the experience lasted. The light softened into an afternoon glow. Once more the breeze rustled the leaves, the birds sang and I could hear a faraway car. I walked on.

The vision transformed me. I stepped from it into a transfigured world; from agnosticism to gnosis. Everything connected.

When first trying to describe the experience I said it was as if I were hearing music and *knew* I was one of the notes.

I had discovered meaning. I have been buffeted and bruised by events, pain and grief since (haven't we all!) but the vision is untarnished.

Believing is seeing!

M. 77 (23)   1136

Father, ex-sailor (*sail* days). Mother Swedish *farm* stock. Education: elementary schools, then self. Wide reading. Preacher poet. Lecturer, varied subjects. One of family of nine.

Religious experience: day school at 6. Sunday School at Welsh Methodist Mission Hall. Became a preacher there at 17.

I was called up to serve in the First World War, but by then I was an uncompromising pacifist, the only one of my family. I was sent first to an NCC unit and then court-martialled for refusing to obey orders and sentenced to two years in prison.

My cell was on the ground floor of one hall. The first fourteen nights I had to sleep on the board bed without a mattress and did not sleep well at all. Moreover, I began to suffer from claustrophobia badly. One night a younger man in the next cell to me – a young Quaker – cracked up badly. His screams caused a commotion and he was taken away. Then it was my turn and I was first on the point of breaking up likewise when the situation *changed* dramatically.

I was praying then and, I think, sobbing too – quietly – when the prison *vanished*. I was looking up at the stars. And at one star in particular, the light of which shot up and outward to form a complete cross. It seemed to say to me, 'By this Sign, Conquer!'

I rolled on to a very sore hip and went off to sleep. Next morning and always thereafter I was utterly happy. Nothing could affect me!

Warders commanded me to 'Take that smile off your face!' Had no effect whatever. My smile was permanent. When one officer on the exercise yard ordered 'Double march', I ran and ran, with a broken shoe on one foot until everyone else had given in and dropped out! And I was never a runner!

From that night I have never doubted the reality of God as some *one*, not an *it* – not an ultimate reality or principle but someone who was *near*. Now at 77 plus, He still is!

I quoted at a Quaker meeting the saying of a Jewish rabbi, 'Three factors are necessary to make a life significant. They are God, a soul and a moment.' I added, when quoting these words, 'The three are always present, but the recognition *not* always. The moment is just the moment of recognition. And *that* may be one or one half of a second, but it will illuminate a whole lifetime and *never* end. That is the Eternal Now which a man, a woman or a child may experience once and for all time. I *did* and I *know it*!'

F. 51 (49) 4138

I was standing at my kitchen sink one evening, looking at the various plants I have on the window-sill, one of which is a spider plant. I was feeling particularly pleased about it because I had managed to salvage it from a much larger one, which had given up the ghost after my mother died.

I began to mentally praise it, when I suddenly became aware that there was a wonderful feeling coming out from the plant and I felt that it was 'loving' me. In fact, I felt that I became it and it became me and that we were all one with the universe. We seemed to be surrounded with 'waves' of 'love', which is the only way I can describe the feeling. It lasted about half a minute and was like nothing else I have ever experienced.

It has made me realize that what St John said, that 'God is Love', was the absolute truth and that that kind of love is unconditional whereas human love isn't.

I later faced an operation quite calmly because I realized it really didn't matter now whether I lived or died, because everything was taken care of and everything was for the best.

I was so glad to read that research is being done into this kind of happening, because if you mention it, people think you're mad!

F. 55 (35)   4267

I was 35 years old at the time and the mother of four children. We lived next to a somewhat crotchety old man, who lived on his own. Whenever we went on holiday, he insisted on having the key of our house 'so that he could keep an eye on things'. As soon as we returned from holiday, he would appear immediately to give us a blow-by-blow account of what had been happening to him in our absence. As you may imagine, this was not always welcome in the throes of unpacking, seeing to the children, etc.!

However, on this particular holiday, he was thwarted, as we did not arrive home until 11 p.m. I fully expected him to appear early the next morning. But 9 a.m. 10 and 11 came and went, and there was still no sign of him. At midday I was in the kitchen, cleaning out the refrigerator, which was full of green mould! I said casually to my husband, 'You'd better look in to see how old C is.' A few minutes later I heard them chatting and laughing in the street outside. 'Good, he's all right then', I thought with relief.

As I said these words to myself, the kitchen and garden were filled with golden light. I became conscious that at the centre of the Universe, and in my garden, was a great pulsing dynamo that ceaselessly poured out love. This love poured over and through me, and I was part of it and it wholly encompassed me. 'Perfectly me, I was perfectly part of perfection.'

The vision was gone in a moment, leaving me with a strong desire to rush out and embrace anyone I could find, including Mr C! At the same time, I had a very strong feeling that the vision was holy and not to be chatted about. Indeed, I did not speak of it except to my husband for some years. Another apprehension was that it was outside time. I also find the words I use to describe it quite inadequate. It was overwhelmingly real, more real than anything I had experienced, although I had been in love, and the feelings after the birth of each of my children had been wonderful. The vision was of a far 'realler' quality. To deny it would be the ultimate sin, blasphemy.

Meditating upon the event, I think the fact that it happened when for once in my life I was altruistically concerned for the well-being of another person is significant. I may also say that I had never before read anything about mystical experience – although I did afterwards, of course!

I wish I could say that I became a miraculously saintly being afterwards. On the contrary, I have gone through a long period of psychological trauma, having to face some hard truths about myself! It is rather as if I had been taken to the top of the mountain, shown a marvellous land, and then been taken down to the bottom of the mountain and been told I must climb to the top if I wish to dwell in the land which I now know exists. I have no excuse now for unloving behaviour towards another – a gift of grace brings awesome responsibility!

M. 55 (28)   947

Although what I want to relate refers to a single 'incident', in a sense it was clearly the culmination of all my previous experience; but just as clearly it was also more than that.

The time was 2.10 a.m. on 5 November. The place, the Western Desert. I was Wireless Officer and a few hours earlier I had realized, by listening to a variety of radio reports, mostly in Morse, that the battle had been won – the breakthrough had come. Although very tired – few of us had had any real sleep for some ten days – I was content to lie on the sand on my back and soak up the unaccustomed silence.

Looking back, I suppose I must have been very exhausted in every way. My regiment had suffered severe casualties and I had lost nearly all of my particular friends. I had had a lot of luck, just two very small flesh wounds, which did not even hurt much. Also I had recently learnt that my new wife, whom I had left at home, was pregnant.

It is not surprising, in the circumstances, that I took thought about 'the meaning of life' – call it what you will. Over the years I had developed some quite strong theories about the existence or otherwise of a god, but they formed a very incomplete jigsaw puzzle and I was keenly aware of the huge gaps in which I hoped might one day become a tenable personal philosophy or religion.

For the first time since before the battle I was lying *on* the ground, rather than in a slit trench or inside a tank or armoured car. The dust of battle, which had obscured the sky, had quite gone, and the stars were enormous and magnificent. A slight breeze came from the warm sea nearby and the air seemed to be slightly perfumed, from what source I could not imagine.

Suddenly – and it really was quite sudden – my train of thought accelerated and vastly improved in quality (I am trying to choose my words carefully to describe what happened). New and convincing ideas came into my mind in a steady torrent, flaws in my existing ideas were illuminated and as I made mental corrections to them the diminishing gaps in the logical sequence were filled by neat, brand-new linking concepts which made a beautiful logical pattern.

I was immediately aware that this was important to me as nothing had been before. The impact was so powerful that for a split second I felt something akin to fear, but this I rejected quickly because, simultaneously, I was enjoying an almost, nay actually, physical thrill of delight. Yes, I think delight is the right word.

What I want to stress most (and this taxes my powers of description) is that a small, everyday, critical part of my brain was standing apart, observing with astonishment what was going on in the rest of my thinking apparatus. How long the experience lasted I hesitate to estimate, but it was probably not more than ten minutes – perhaps less.

After only a few seconds 'I' realized that no effort of mine was involved in what, for me, was a highly superior piece of thinking and, moreover, it was taking place with an energetic *authority* which was unlike anything I had ever known about myself (I was always a cautious, doubtful thinker). That small watch-dog part of my brain marvelled at this as it happened. This ability to experience thought on two quite distinct levels simultaneously is something I have never heard mentioned as being possible, and I feel inadequate to describe it! It has never recurred.

There was no specific 'religious' aspect in the pattern of ideas which presented itself to me. It had to do with man's (my) position in relation to the universe; it dealt with eternity, which became readily understandable; with infinity, which faced one with ultimate fear unless the next stage in the logic was appreciated – strangely enough (as I thought then) to do with the relationship between the sexes. And so on, until, as suddenly as it had started, the train of thought paused, at a very reasonable point, and added, as a definite statement, 'That's quite enough to be going on with.'

I remember taking a deep breath and exclaiming aloud 'You can say that again!'

Years later, discussing this with one of the few (very) friends sensitive enough for me to talk to about such an intensely personal experience, I learnt the rather pompous expression 'euphoria of cerebration'. I did have actual pleasurable thrills running across underneath my skull, almost like a cold shower in hot weather, but, as it were, in a higher octave and champagne, not water.

I stood up and stretched, rested and elated. I am as sure as anyone can be about such things that I had not been asleep; in fact, I had never been so wide awake, so conscious. I crawled into my armoured car, switched on the light and made notes on the backs of signal forms, because I knew it was important not to forget.

I will not try to sell you the philosophy which grew out of this experience. For me, it works. Not complete of course. It would probably crumble to dust if it ever finally crystallized out. Growth or atrophy.

The point I must make is this: I find it impossible to believe that what happened originated inside me. Perhaps, unwittingly, I tapped some universal source of knowledge. The power was there, like a fire hose. God? What's in a name? And yet, I felt tremendous *gratitude* immediately afterwards – and one only feels gratitude, surely, to a person. Or was that just a conditioned reflex from school bible training?

Years afterwards it occurred to me that perhaps something similar happened to those early prophets who 'heard the voice of God'. Theirs must have been a hard, dangerous life, often in desert places. I make no such claim, but they may have expressed it so, with their less sophisticated outlook. It was not a voice which I could hear with my ears. It was as if another mind was using my brain, and the ideas came in the sequence in which words are used aloud.

Certainly I enjoyed a long moment of deep insight which has never lost its validity for me. I had a great sense at the time of the beauty of form of what was presented to me, quite apart from the content.

F. ? (?)   4664

The night had been long and for me agonizing. How was I to know what labour pains were really like? This was my first pregnancy – I hadn't anticipated the pains to be so breathtaking and uncontrollable.

I had done the 'breathing' exercises and hardly let out a groan – I had done all that was expected of me. In doing so I thought I could control everything as I had been taught in the childbirth classes. But nothing had prepared me for the reality of labour pains. I felt overwhelmed by what was happening and wanted to get up and walk away from the situation. But I couldn't.

At last the moment of birth came. They gave me a mirror and I watched as the baby's head appeared first, then one shoulder, then another, until her whole slippery body slithered out. I waited until they told me what sex the baby was. They showed her to me and laid her down beside me on the table. 'Why doesn't she cry?' I wanted to know, as I watched her just staring and blinking up at the ceiling. The midwife smiled and gave her a gentle prod and she let out a squawk. She looked so small, this perfectly formed being with tiny finger- and toe-nails and little eyelashes. I could hardly believe that I was responsible for producing such a creature and that she was mine.

It was the moments that followed I call my 'religious experience'. I remember saying, 'This is what is happening all over the world at this very moment.' As I said this, I felt a tremendous sense of both wonder at the present moment and unity with humanity. I was no longer an individual. I felt totally and deeply absorbed and immersed, just for a few moments and in a momentous event – a universal but unique experience, giving birth.

I was no longer an Englishwoman giving birth in an English hospital. I was a woman in India, Africa or China or as a part of history. I had taken part in the universal cycle of birth and death and in the struggle for life. It was a totally self-forgetting experience, as I felt part of the immediate whole. I was caught in an intense timeless moment in which I lost my own sense of self-identity.

F. 58 (44) 4182

We came back from holiday to find that my mother had died unexpectedly and no one had been able to get in touch with us. I was then 44, very happily married, with three children, and a believing but somewhat detached Anglican. I can never remember a time when I doubted the existence of God, though I have not been able yet to feel the great compelling power which the person of Jesus exerts on so many. Belief in Christ as the Spirit of God is the nearest I can come to it.

It is difficult to write what came next. Anything one does write is totally inadequate and I was too shaken and disturbed to do so at the time. My remembrance now is inevitably coloured by subsequent reading of mystical literature, but at that time I had not the slightest idea that such literature existed and had never come across it. All I can truthfully say now, after several years, is that at some point in the next few days – even before the funeral, I think – I had the most shattering experience of my entire life. I believe it was during a sleepless night, but it seems to have been an experience entirely out of time as we accept the notion. Without any sense perception (except that I do seem to recollect an impression of light and darkness), I was made aware of a Reality beyond anything that my own mind could have conceived. And that Reality was a total love of all things in heaven and earth. 'It' enclosed and accepted every thing and every creature: there was no distinction of its love between the star, the saint and the torturer. All were 'kept' by this Power, and loved by it. I understood – then at least – the phrases 'I am that I am' and what I later read as 'the coincidence of opposites'. 'It' is Eternal Being.

There was much more, but somewhere in this time of dark night a symbol (a morning glory flower, as it happens) arose – from my subconscious, I suppose – which brought me a tremendous relief and comfort. I subsequently read of such happenings in Jung but, again, knew nothing of them at the time.

It was all overwhelming and psychologically terrifying; I was very frightened at the time that I was going mad. I quite accept that all this might well seem a natural reaction to shock and grief and guilt, and a self-induced comfort in a time of emotional and physical turmoil.

For myself I did not doubt then, and have never doubted since, that I was put in touch with that ultimate reality for which we use the shorthand 'God'.

F. ? (fifteen years ago)   4278

I would like to tell you of an experience I had some fifteen years ago in Africa, where we then lived.

My husband and I were relaxing over our customary evening drink, and the *Sunday Times* crossword, when suddenly I was made conscious of a wonderful feeling of upliftment. A glow seemed to come over me (no, not the whisky!) and I asked my husband not to speak for a moment. A sense of power surged through me and, somewhat bewildered, I tried to channel my thoughts into universal love. Certainly, I had perception of power beyond and greater than self. Slowly, the sensation faded away and my thoughts came back to normal. Disappointingly, I was tongue-tied when I endeavoured to explain what had happened, to my husband, as he did not think along those lines at all. It was too precious an experience to tell to just anybody, so I kept it to myself for a very long time.

Being a Sunday night, with no staff, I went into the kitchen (partly because I wanted to be by myself) and cooked a positively inspired supper!

Now, when I become low-spirited, I try to look back on my experience and to realize that there must be something above our mundane life.

F. ? (?)   4614

I was looking after the Friends Meeting House high on a spur of the forest, and sleeping on a camp bed in the sitting-room of the dwelling next door. One night I awoke slowly at about one o'clock to a feeling of absolute safety and happiness; everything in the world around me seemed to be singing 'All is very well'. After an almost unbelieving few minutes I got up and went to the window and saw the valley filled with the love of God, flowing and spreading from the roadside and the few houses of the village. It was as though a great source of light and love and goodness was there along the valley, absolutely true and unchangeable. I went outside and looked down over the hedge, and the light and assurance were most truly there; I looked and looked, and, to be honest, I was not thankful, as I should have been, but trying to absorb the awareness of safety and joy so deeply that I would never forget it.

Next day I visited a paralysed, indeed dying, doctor, and as I waited in his kitchen for him to be ready to see me, I picked up an old *Reader's Digest* that his housekeeper was reading, open at an article on just such religious experiences as I had had the previous night. This convinced me I was quite sane and I even told the doctor something of my experience.

F. ? (seventeen years ago)   2138

The experience I am relating here took place in the summer. I had spent the weekend with friends and because of a sudden train strike I had to return by a bus which deposited me half a mile from my home in the middle of the night: it could have been 1.30 a.m. I began to walk across the common. It was quite dark of course – street lamps had all been switched off, and there was no traffic – but the night was warm and still, and the sky full of stars. I had no particular feeling beyond a slight nervousness about being out so late in a lonely spot; on the whole I think I was enjoying the walk.

I had nearly reached my mother's house when I suddenly realized that the whole sky was alive with sound. Out of the deep silence grew a whole orchestration – not of music, but of a harmonious blending of sounds, as though an infinite number of radio transmitters were emitting signals, each one with its own unique pitch and rhythm of pulsation. There was no melody and no form: I just knew that what I was hearing was the music of the spheres, something that has no beginning and no ending, and the grandeur and simplicity of this filled me with amazement and delight. At the same time I vividly recalled the taste of painted metal and my memory tugged me straight back to the nursery in another house, where, night after night (though I had totally forgotten it until that moment) I had stood as a tiny child, sucking the bars at the window and listening to the stars.

I arrived at my mother's house and went indoors; upstairs in my bedroom I could still hear the stars singing, and they continued to do so until I reluctantly went to sleep. I have never heard this sound again, though I have often longed to do so for the joy and satisfaction it brought. Perhaps the oddest part of this experience was that it felt so normal.

Soon afterwards I began work on an army training film dealing with radio relay, and I took the opportunity of questioning the officer acting as adviser. He assured me that stars do in fact emit radio signals, and he explained patiently and at length why human ears are unable to receive these signals. I did not tell him of my experience – but I have shared it with friends from time to time, and one close friend told me that he had had a very similar experience late one night while serving as a naval officer in the Red Sea.

F. ? (twenty years ago)   2611

On the way home from a walk in the countryside I passed the house where one of the rooms was used as a church (RC). I popped in to say a prayer. I wasn't feeling religious; in fact, I felt particularly emotionally dry. As I was praying I felt as if I was talking to a wall, as if nobody was there or listening to me. As happens often, I felt a bit frustrated and tried to force myself to feel a bit of emotion. Instead of *feeling* anything, I left my body, like popping through a hole in a wall, suspended just below the ceiling. I was aware that I had left my body and, although I felt wonderful and right, without thinking I panicked to get back to my body. It was like swimming against the current to get back, but the whole thing probably didn't last longer than a second or two. I was rather shaken and went straight home. I didn't see anything during this experience nor felt a tremendous emotion. I didn't tell anybody, except my husband a while later. I never experienced anything like this before or after.

When I say *I* left my body and not 'my soul left my body', this is because it felt like this; one thinks of one's soul as something detached, like a heart, but it was me and not something abstract.

F. ? (two years ago) 4755

Two years ago I had an odd experience which I have scarcely mentioned because the response (even from my husband) has been embarrassment tinged with worry about my mental state. I could see the thoughts 'neurotic' and 'menopausal symptom' forming in the eyes of those I told (except in the case of my youngest son, who airily dismissed it as an 'OOBE' – something I had never heard of until he showed me a magazine on the paranormal about 'out-of-body-experiences').

The 'happening' was in church one Sunday morning when, instead of paying much attention to the service, I was worrying about the things which preoccupy most mothers of three adolescents (e.g., would my eldest son fail his A levels/fall off his motorbike/sleep with his girl-friend/take drugs/dye his hair pink, etc., etc.).

Suddenly I was 'taken out of myself' (I can't think of any other way to express it, but I felt disembodied) and taken up and felt that I was at the edge of a tremendous crowd surrounding a bright light. The ones nearest were drenched in the light and all I wanted ('yearned for' would be nearer) was to be drawn into the light too. There was no 'Christ figure' – just light.

Suddenly I knew I was back 'inside' myself, but was left with a feeling of peace, which lasted for several weeks. *Not* that the things that I was worrying about would not happen, but a feeling of assurance that even if they did, it didn't matter – ultimately all would be well.

And that's it. It doesn't sound very exciting written down, but it was real enough. I was not asleep (in fact, we were standing at the time) and I was not day-dreaming. I *do* day-dream, but this was completely different – much as I would like to, I am quite unable to recapture the experience. I was not on drugs and my health was good. I could find no explanation for what I felt was a glimpse of another dimension of existence.

F. 56 (?)   **2733**

The ultimate proof to me of life after death and the love of God
came just after the birth of my daughter.

It had been a long and difficult birth and I was very exhausted.
As nurse helped me to sit up, I remember saying 'I do feel funny'.
Everything whirled and blackness formed a tunnel, a long, long
tunnel with an opening at the other end which glowed with a bright
light.

Down, down into the whirling blackness. It seemed a long time
before I reached the opening and found myself floating gently in
a soft warm mist, all golden as with sunlight, soft music and a
feeling of complete happiness, and such peace that passes all
understanding was mine; faces came out of the mist, smiled and
faded away.

I seemed to be fully conscious and knowing that I had 'died' yet
I lived. God's plan of good death had no sting.

Then came the remembrance of the baby – who would look after
her if I stayed?

My next reaction was to pain: my face stung as the doctor
slapped first one side, then the other – hard.

As I opened my eyes he greeted me with 'You naughty girl,
you've given me the biggest fright of my life.' He looked startled
when I answered, 'Don't begrudge me that: it was absolutely
wonderful.'

I still feel *very* grateful and humble for this experience, certainly
have no fear of death, knowing it is as simple as walking from one
room to another.

M. 68 (?)   **398**

. . . a normal but very active lad, reared on a farm in the USA. I
loved the outdoors and would at times run as fast as possible just
for the fun of it.

Once, out in a field on a well-travelled pathway across a
neighbour's farm of low, rolling hills, I was thinking deeply on the
subject of Jesus as the son of God and some of the miracles
recorded in the Bible.

I lifted my eyes heavenward and seemed to see Jesus there in the clouds before me. I began running toward Him as fast as I could run. There came into my mind this question: is this the hour, am I to go now? As long as I kept my eyes and my mind on Him, I kept rising, running very fast but not tiring at all. When I realized that I was several feet above ground and had passed over a wagon-gate across the path or roadway, I became afraid I might fall. The clouds covered Him from my view. I looked Earthward and was soon back down running on the ground. No longer was He visible in the clouds and I was once again an Earth-bound creature as before.

F. 28 (13) 630

I have only had one such 'feeling', but it was so strong that I was convinced that I had had a message from God. It happened about fifteen years ago. I was absolutely miserable. The cause of my unhappiness could not have been very important, because I can't even remember why I was feeling this way, but I think it was something at school. I am sure, though, that it was something blown out of all proportion by an adolescent mind. I was more than half seriously thinking of ways of committing suicide, but one night I had a dream that I was going to die. I knew in this dream that I was going to be killed and in the near future, and that there was nothing I could do about it. I knew then that I didn't want to die and, still in the dream, I implored and prayed as hard as I knew how to be allowed to live. After a time I had a wonderful feeling of peace and I knew everything would be all right. The next morning, and ever since, I was sure that I would never have such thoughts again.

My parents were not church-goers, and I'm afraid neither am I nor my husband. I have been christened in the Church of England, but have never been confirmed. I do strongly believe in a God, but who or what God is, I just don't know.

F. ? (13)   **4110**

Something came to me when I was 13 years old. I saw a picture of a pile of Jews' bodies waiting to be bulldozed into a mass grave in Germany during the Second World War. Of course I was shocked, but the 'whatever it is' took the opportunity to pound my brain from the inside for twelve hours. I can remember thinking 'I don't know what you want. What am I to do?' I was not confused or frightened, just sort of 'taken over'. At the end of the twelve hours I thought – though I can't remember why – that maybe I should choose a career as a doctor. Suddenly the 'whatever it is' vacated my head and allowed me to return to normal.

That was it really. People were a bit surprised at my career choice, because I was rather a 'slow starter'. I plodded a bit harder with school work, but not really enough to justify the sharp increase in success I experienced at O level. I had a minor set-back when one of my A-level grades was too low for entry to medical school, but it was only a temporary loss of confidence. 'Whatever it is' can cope with well-intentioned plodders apparently, and I got in the next year.

I used to wonder if this thing that gives me strength had some sort of mission for me. I doubt this, as despite a certain knowledge that God exists, I cannot find him/her in religion of any sort (not that I've tried very much). In fact, I prefer not to think about it at all in case it goes away. It's nice not to have to worry about bad times. *It* arrives when necessary, sometimes in the most unexpected situations.

F. ? (two years ago)   **4325**

I am a Piscean and have been told as such that I am quite perceptive, i.e., in my own terms I do tend to be able to read people and sometimes know when the telephone is going to ring or what those close to me are about to say; these, of course, are just a few things.

But what I wish to write to you about is something which I found quite frightening at the time it happened. There have been many occasions in my life when I have visited a place and felt deep down inside that I have been there before, but on the occasion I wish to mention I have never been so afraid in my life.

Two years ago while travelling by car through Europe my husband, daughter and two friends of ours stopped off on our journey home in a major town to spend the night. Our friends were shown to their room and my husband, daughter and I to another. There was a single bed for our daughter, then aged 15 years, and one double for my husband and me. We had all been travelling many hours and were hot, sticky and tired. On entering the room I felt a most terrible chill, a fear I had never known. I am afraid I cannot put into words what exactly I felt, only to say that some terrible presence was in this room also. I said nothing to my husband or daughter, as we were all so tired, but I do tend to feel things in other places, e.g., houses we visit, etc.

We washed and all fell into bed. I could not sleep, would not sleep, though I felt my eyes would burst. My husband fell quickly into a deep sleep, as did my daughter. On so doing, I pulled her bed close to ours so that it touched. I felt the need to protect them both and because of such sat up all night. On the bedside table next to me was a Bible; although I am of the Jewish faith and not religious, this, even so, made me feel at that time very close to God. (I do pray every night, even walking in the street, even in the bathroom, whenever I feel the need.) I do not believe one has to be religious to speak with God.

But the Bible made me feel strong, made me feel that whatever was in this room I could fight and that God would fight alongside me. The strangest thing is that after a couple of hours I felt the need to get out of the bed, although I felt frozen, and to take a cover and lie on the floor at the foot of the beds. I lay there for a moment or two, but felt an even greater fear and sprang, almost jumping, back into bed and there I stayed until dawn, when I quickly drew the curtains and woke everyone up, laughingly saying, 'We have a long journey.' Incidentally I left the bathroom light on in our room all night long.

The above may not be psychic, it may not be a religious or spiritual happening, but I have felt this need to write to someone or speak with someone that might understand how exactly I felt at that particular time.

The experience will never leave me, for in that room I felt that something really terrible had once happened, something like a murder. That night will stay with me for ever, such was my fear for those I loved.

M. 45 (?)   248

On the last evening of a convention three of us set out at about 10.15 p.m. for a walk through a small wood which led to a village on the other side. N, one of the party, started to tell the story of his life ... On joining the Forces he had missed the influence of home and fell into bad company, unable to resist temptation.

As N finished his story there was silence. I sat with my eyes closed, wondering how I, as one of the convention leaders, could help the young fellow. What happened next was over in a very short space of time. Breaking through the silence, and crashing through the darkness with tremendous power came my voice: 'In the name of the Lord Jesus Christ, depart.' Immediately N let out a half shout and fell towards me. He said afterwards, 'At those words "in the name of the Lord Jesus Christ" I saw a black form appear from somewhere at my feet and vanish into the wood and, at the same time, something indescribable left me.'

I felt an urgency for prayer; that if N did not pray, something would happen to him. It was at this point an event occurred so dreadful that since I have prayed that it should never happen again. It seemed as if horrifying pandemonium had been let loose; as if all the powers of Hell were concentrated in that spot in the wood. I saw numbers of black shapes, blacker than the night, moving about and seeking to come between myself and N, who I was gripping hard. I saw three demon spirits, perhaps more, between N and myself. These shapes were intelligences. They were different one from another. Each had a personality of its own. They began to buffet me, not striking me physically, but thrusting me backwards in spirit away from N so as to make me recoil, perhaps from fear, and so loose my hold. Two other demon spirits, about shoulder high, were just behind me. One on my right, the other on my left. These two were moving about with a swaying, menacing up-and-down motion, such as boxers use when seeking an opening for attack.

Again I felt an intense urgency for prayer, particularly for N. 'Pray, N' I called to him, but the poor fellow could do nothing but sob. With my hands on his shoulders, I cried: 'The blood of Jesus Christ cleanseth from all sin.' Again and again, I repeated the phrase. I did not notice T was silent until he said 'What a horrible atmosphere.' 'Pray, T,' I commanded, 'pray with us.' Together we cried with a loud voice, 'The blood of Jesus Christ cleanseth from all sin.'

Then, after a pause, in a colossal voice, such as I have never heard before or since, came a verse from scripture through my lips in terrifying power. The words were forced out of my mouth. 'I give to my sheep eternal life, they shall never perish, neither shall any pluck them out of my hand.' I was left absolutely gasping after this. My mouth had been stretched open wider and wider, as if the words were too big for my lips to utter. I then led with the Lord's Prayer. For T this was a real climax; he saw nothing, but again felt the atmosphere change. As we reached the words 'deliver us from evil: for thine is the kingdom the *power and the glory*,' the feeling of power was immense; the atmosphere was charged with a living presence, impossible to describe. Then everything grew quiet. The air seemed soft and pleasant, as if angel voices were singing, as if a battle had ended or a great storm had blown itself out. N whispered, 'Praise God. Oh, what joy.'

We made our way back to the conference centre. N could not wait until morning to share the news of his deliverance. Quite independently, N told of how he had seen seven black forms emerge from the trees in the wood and how he felt some power pushing him forward out of my grip. Luke 11: 24, 26.

F. ? (?)   2674

After the sudden death of a 4½-year-old son, I found no comfort in anything or anyone; the Church seemed powerless to help me, as did the medical profession. I could not go out of the flat I was living in at that time and, although I tried very hard, I could see nothing but blackness and an intense longing to die. One morning I was dusting, tidying, the usual household chores, when I smelled the most wonderful garden flowers. It is difficult to describe the smell I mean – rather like a garden after rain. Being of a somewhat practical mind in such things, I looked around for the source of the smell. There were no flowers in the flat, certainly none outside, no perfumed polishes or toilet things in use. Then I sat down and for the first time since my son died I felt peaceful inside. I believe this was God's comfort; my son felt very near and I no longer felt alone.

All I can tell you now is that I have no fear of what we call death. To me it will be shedding the material life for a spiritual life and although I have had no great revelations, I shall try to live according to His divine plan and be ready to leave when He is ready for me.

F. 71 (66)   **2026**

When I learned that my aunt (mother's sister), who was one of our family, aged 84 years was a cancer victim, I was appalled at the thought of having to nurse her. Now retired, I was even to devote myself entirely to my nursing duties, which were to last for three months.

One night I had settled my patient for the night and sat down in my chair near her bed, with my back to the window. Why, I do not know, but my eyes seemed drawn to the corner of the room. There, at the top of the wall shone a small light, which slowly grew in size and brilliance. I could not withdraw my gaze but I had no sense of fear. I determined to be quite practical and made myself look out of the window, thinking that an outside light might be reflected in the bedroom, but there was no outside light. I sat down again and kept my eyes on the light. I have never, before or after, felt such a sense of peace and comfort. I felt a powerful presence in the bedroom and I knew that I would be given divine strength to carry on with my duty to the end. I felt an exhilaration, a peace and well-being and I knew that I had been given a manifestation of God's care for me, unworthy though I was. I went to sleep, calm and reassured, knowing that the burden was no longer mine.

There was an unexpected sequel to my experience.

On the following night, when I had again attended to my patient,

I noticed that she did not, as usual, close her eyes. I followed her gaze and was surprised to realize that she was staring up at the very place where the light had shone for me. I asked my aunt what she was looking at. She replied, 'Nothing.'

I said, 'Come on. Tell me. What do you see up there?'

She replied, 'I'm not going to tell you. It's a secret.'

My aunt died a few days later. I am convinced that we were both, however unworthy, privileged to be granted this manifestation of divine help in our hour of need.

F. 65 (?)   2062

One night when I was saying my prayers I suddenly felt a great light all around me and I seemed to be walking or rather floating up between rows of figures towards something of intense brightness, and a voice said, 'Go your way in peace and your ways shall be shown unto you.'

But the light was like nothing on Earth, it was all around and uplifted me with an indescribable feeling.

Since that day I have not worried about any decision I may have had to make, as I know that the way that has opened for me has been the right one and always will be.

F. 52 (44)   4230

I had been ill and was at a low ebb but not near death or anything like – I had recovered from whooping cough but been left with asthma. It was mid-afternoon. Fully awake, I lay on my son's bed with the window open and it looks over roof-tops to a tiny view of the moors. I was completely empty of any thought.

I was suddenly bathed in a waterfall of pure light, a feeling that everything was at one – everything around me, plus me, plus *some*thing else. It was seconds only in time, but yet time-less. As I lay there I thought 'This is the Holy Trinity'. I can only say it was as if this Holy Trinity was pure silk in content. I did not feel that I wanted to dwell on it, nor did I feel that I wanted to tell anyone, not even my husband, but I was left with a feeling of peace and warmth in my heart that has never left me. And although I have since had family trauma that has made me feel really ill, I have this certainty of inner peace without withdrawal.

I do not know if I am changed as a person, but I do flinch and I am really hurt when anyone I know cannot see some thread of goodness in anyone or anything and I feel for the real hurt that this causes to Christ our Lord God. In every respect I am still living my life as I have, being a wife, mother, a member of local institutions.

F. ? (two years ago)   4057

I am not religious. I think I am level-headed and I work as a legal secretary.

Two years ago my father-in-law was extremely ill with cancer. For the last eight days of his life my husband and I stayed with him almost continuously and he died holding our hands. No one close to me had ever died before and this affected me deeply.

Since his death I have felt him near every day but could only see him as he was when he died, which was extremely distressing.

In October last year his brother L was also dying of cancer. My husband and I went out for a ride on the motor bike. Coming home it was about 6.25 p.m. and almost completely dark. We came up over a hill and I had an extremely strange feeling. I looked over towards the fields and there was a brilliant blue light, dark blue but bright. The sky was blue. It's hard to describe the colour. I am not sure whether I imagined it in my mind but I don't think so: I saw in amongst the blue my late father-in-law's face, a very peaceful face. I then felt his brother die and come to him. It was very peaceful. We must have passed this spot in a matter of seconds but it seemed like minutes. Incidentally, this blue sky highlighted three bare trees, which stood out.

When we got to my mother's house at about 6.30 p.m. I got off the bike and announced to my husband, mother and father that L had just died. Whether it was because of the way I said it and acted that surprisingly no one laughed and they believed me. We then waited for the telephone to ring to announce his death. At 8 p.m. the call came and the timing was exactly right: he had died when I saw what I have described above right to the minute. Discussing it later the spot where I had experienced this was in a direct line with the house in which he died.

From that day on I can now see my father-in-law as he was and not the man I had seen dying.

People I have told have not laughed but I still find it embarrassing.

F. 59 (25) 4410

I was living in a hostel. On a Saturday afternoon I was lying on my bed feeling depressed and lonely. Although I wanted to get up and go out to buy some cigarettes, I felt unable to move bacause of the feeling of depression. Instead, I continued to lie on the bed and began to wish fervently and with all my strength that I had some religion to help me. Within a few minutes a very bright light appeared in the opposite corner of the room near to the ceiling and I heard a voice say 'Take up your bed and walk.'

I am a graduate, married now to a scientist, and have never suffered from hallucinations of any sort. I am still not particularly religious, but this experience has stayed with me in complete detail for over thirty years.

F. 43 (33) 4114

Ten years ago I had what could only be described as a nervous breakdown. I was 33 and depressed. I was afraid of dying and all the other symptoms of this illness. I was alone one day and a voice spoke to me. The voice came from within but was clear and distinct. It simply said, 'Carry on as you are and you are dead.' From that moment I started to get better and grew strong in mind and body. I feel a new person. I find I am able to help others with similar problems. The strange thing is though I have not heard the voice since, I feel that something or someone is watching over me and having a large influence on my thoughts and life. I also have this very strong feeling that we, mankind that is, are a part of something far beyond our comprehension. My life has new meaning and purpose.

F. 35 (22)   640

I was sent to Sunday school and church until about the age of 12, when I was allowed to stop. The teaching was all in terms of 'being saved' and 'washed in the blood of the lamb' and was expressed entirely in clichés, which were never explained and therefore exasperated me. But at least the idea of 'God' was introduced.

In my adolescence I described myself as an atheist, with no very clear notion of what this entailed. Inconsistently enough, I also formulated the thought that if there was a God, I hated him. Which will indicate that my adolescence was unhappy and difficult and became increasingly so as I approached my twenties.

My home life became increasingly miserable and the desire to find some kind of explanation of our existence on this earth and some power which might turn me outwards from myself to love of others, which my reading indicated to me as the only way of salvation, reached a quite excruciating pitch.

I was 22 and all this went on hiddenly. I fell into exhausted sleep each night and woke in tears at the thought of the tormented day that lay ahead.

One night, in desperation, I knelt by my bed and thought 'O God, help me' – little more. And immediately I was flooded with such a sense of being touched by an almighty and beneficent power as is impossible to describe. I went to sleep filled with joy.

When I woke, I mentally reached out to that same being and found him/her/it still there.

In the weeks that followed I nervously told a very few friends and approached the minister of the nearest church, who suggested I read the Gospels, which I did.

I have called myself a Christian since and have become part of the Christian Church because the life of Jesus and His declarations about himself and the Comforter seem the best objective framework into which to fit my subjective experience, but my faith has never been as certain and unquestionable as that of many another I have met.

Whatever may be my state now or in the future, the experience did happen and I'm certain that whatever anyone says 'Axioms in philosophy are not axioms until they are proved upon our pulses.'

F. 50 (?)   2524

Many years ago I had a very painful and frightening ordeal to go through. Thank God, I had always believed in prayer and knelt to pray for what must have been nearly two hours.

There were tears everywhere; I felt weak and so alone. Then I truly felt a brightness around me and a firm hand on my shoulder; words just can't explain it, but I knew I was not alone.

Afterwards nothing had changed. I still had the ordeal to go through, but not alone. I came through it a better person because of it.

F. 92 (16)   4761

I was only 16 at the time. I had an older sister, who possessed the biting Irish tongue that can be so devastating and I had been subjected to it all my life. On one occasion I was desperate; without appealing to Almighty God, I was suddenly conscious of a brilliant light and such a consoling message of encouragement given me by God the Father, not Jesus. Of course, this was understood subjectively, but it was as realistic as any other voice. I have never forgotten it and because of it, have no doubts about the existence of God, in spite of the aberrations of His Church! I am nearly 92, so the experience really stuck.

M. & F. 81 (26)   3015

This happened in the year when Lord Derby was calling for army recruits, before conscription, for World War I. We were 'boy and girl' friends, and married when the war was behind us. My husband-to-be knew he would have to enlist and he dreaded the idea, but did not want to be a conscript, so decided to join the Derby scheme that summer.

It was Saturday evening, a glorious evening, with a most brilliant moon, when he asked *my* opinion about this 'joining up', but I refused, as I said if anything happened to him, I should always blame myself! We were on a country lane near my home, now built up, but then pasture land on both sides, which I knew well on each side of this road.

As we walked along, scarcely speaking, as the decision was little nearer, we suddenly saw a brilliance most unusual, even more than the loveliest moon I have ever seen: there was an opening in the stone wall, with much more light than the moon, the width of a farmyard gate, which I knew a gate did not exist for several yards further down the road. Then a figure emerged, a most brilliant sight. We were both speechless, but not afraid, it was so beautiful. The figure, Jesus Christ, glided on to the centre of the road while we were on the rough pavement. We were spellbound as the figure walked up and we were walking down. We could see the white gown with a broad, twisted girdle around his waist, knotted and falling down his left side. The figure glided along, but we could see no feet, and as it got nearer, we tried to make out his face features, but could not, and as it got level with us, it gradually faded away from the bottom of the gown up to the head, and it had vanished!

When we got down to the 'wall opening', it was the solid wall, as I knew it for many years, further down, and it had got to near midnight; but, still, we never spoke to each other, we were spellbound! When we got to my home, as he was about to leave me, we at last spoke, cross-questioned each other on what we had seen, without a hint on the matter, each and every answer coincided. We still remember every detail, but our views on religion have deepened; although, still, we are not *too* religious.

When I got in, home, I told my mother about this strange happening, and her remark, 'Oh! If he goes to be a soldier, he will come back all right!' Funnily enough, he got a 'nasty packet' of 'poison gas' out in France one night when sleeping. He was sent to hospital for treatment for six months, then back on service, and left the army A1, we are thankful to say, when war ended.

F. 77 (thirty years ago) 2720

What I am about to relate happened nearly thirty years ago, but the remembrance of it is still vividly clear to my mind.

I was busily occupied one morning in cooking the lunch and with no other thoughts in mind, when suddenly there was a blinding flash of light and standing at my side was a white-robed figure. I knew it was Christ when I saw the pierced hands and feet, but did not see his face. The amazing brightness all around me was indescribable and I was filled with such *overwhelming* joy that I cannot find words to express all I felt. It was something quite out of this world. I did not hear any voice but just had the conscious feeling that something very wonderful was happening to me. After a few moments the Vision and the Brightness left me, but not the joy. Friends remarked about the happiness in my face a fortnight after it happened.

F. 77 (42) 2012

Thirty-five years ago, when living and working in East London, I became tired and discouraged by a seemingly futile struggle against the poverty and squalor in which brave and uncomplaining people lived with some dignity and even optimism.

I went one afternoon along a dismal little street to conduct a Mothers' Meeting, held in the dark basement hall of a church.

The street disappeared and I found myself standing in a brown schoolroom, or so it seemed, empty except for forms lining the walls. A beautiful white-robed messenger sat on one of the forms, and I saw through the window a sunlit garden ablaze with flowers.

So I said to the messenger, 'Could I go out into the garden?' and with a radiant smile came the answer, 'Of course you can. It is all your Father's house.'

I found myself still walking along that dirty little street, but lifted into a new world by a vision which has stayed with me over the years. In every grief and crisis, this truth has been my guide and inspiration. I fear no evil because nothing but good can come to me while I am everywhere and at all times in my Father's house.

F. ? (one year ago)   2497

I lost my husband in January after forty-eight years of marriage. He had a stroke three years before he died and as time went on he got worse and I had a lot to do for him. When I had lost him, my life seemed empty and I got very depressed and ill. One afternoon in July I went into the kitchenette to make myself a cup of tea, but before I could do it, a heavy weight was lifted off my shoulders. I put my hands together and said 'Thank you, Lord.' Then a very fine cloak came down from my shoulders. I put my hands together again and said 'The Holy Spirit, the Comforter.' It was a beautiful experience. I have got well of myself and it has proved uplifting and has never left me; I don't think it ever will. Thank God, I have never lost my faith in Him.

M. 75 (some weeks ago)   4365

I would like to describe in simple terms a spiritual experience I had a few weeks ago, while entering this home for the elderly, recovering from the shock of my wife's death from cancer. We had been happily married for forty-three years. This religious experience was not in the least sensational. I was in my bedroom. There was a sound of great silence and stillness and the presence of God, with me hugging him in devotion and love around the waist and a feeling that all is well and underneath are the everlasting arms. This is the only such experience I have ever had in my life. I know it's valid and authentic. There was only a sense of serenity and love and nothing to provoke it.

F. ? (?)   2010

My husband died on a coach at 10.30 p.m. and the police informed me at 1.30 a.m. We were a very loving husband and wife, and, although I am resilient by nature, I was emotionally shattered.

When the police left I wanted to be on my own to wrestle with the situation. My heart started to pound and I thought I must surely die. I endured the agony until 4.30 a.m. and was lying on a divan in my breakfast room.

To my amazement and wonder, the window at the foot of the divan was flooded with a wondrous gold light – the colour of 22-carat gold. I was so astonished that my heart gained control and I fell into a dreamless sleep until 7.30 a.m., when I was more able to face the shock.

F. 43 (22) 4092

Childhood

Secure. Happy. Presbyterian background. I recall many times and in seemingly unrelated circumstances when I was overcome with a feeling of great 'inner excitement and joy' and a desire to 'hug the world'.

Adolescence

My adolescence was a most trying and sad time, full of questions about the meaning of suffering, life, death, religion and God.

A summer evening

Alone in my room, feeling extremely desperate about the seeming foolishness of life, I asked, out loud, that 'If there was a God, could He help?' I was immediately overwhelmed by the feeling of a Presence/Light/Love, all around; it seemed everywhere, I really can't explain. It appeared to last for a minute or two, although I can't be sure. I lost all sense of time. I was left with an indescribable feeling of peace and joy.

This moment completely changed my life. Everything, suddenly seemed to make sense.

Now, in middle age, I still look back to those few moments as the most real and important in my life. I am firmly convinced in the reality of God (called by whatever name) and the power of prayer. I have an inner certainty that life, even under the most tragic circumstances, is good. Even more so now than in childhood, I feel a great love for the world and everyone in it.

F. 31 (?)   **4440**

I had just finished my Master's (in psychology) when I had an illness and went to London for my treatment. I am married and have two sons.

I had always believed in God, but hadn't felt Him and Christ so much within me until my illness. I was filled with God so much so that I saw Him wherever I looked, especially in London. I had gone to London with the fear of the amputation of my leg, due to a wrong diagnosis. Thanks to God, I found the best and most humane doctors at the hospital and they said there was no risk of amputation and there is no damage worth mentioning on my leg now, though I had a long radiotherapy. Maybe it was the great churches of London or the beautiful pictures of our saviour Jesus Christ in art galleries that made me be filled with such overpowering excitement and joy. Whatever it was, I thought these feelings could best be expressed in a poem. How God was in me, how God was in London and how much I do miss all of these.

> In a dreary evening
> From a window at my hospital
> I raised my eyes up . . . up . . .,
> To His grey and wide sky.
> I felt Him in my whole self.
> His overpowering strength
> Enthralled my mind and my body
> Enthroned in my heart
> Because
> God was in the Thames
> Flowering gloriously.
> God was in the Big Ben
> Standing All Mighty.
> God was in the Westminster Bridge
> So hilariously.
> He was in the flashing light
> of His Heaven.
> So powerful and yet so tenderly.
> He was in the rain
> Pounding on His Earth
> So harsh and yet so vigorously
> And He was in my tears

So bitter and yet so soothingly
So comfortingly, lovingly
That I somehow knew.
Knew He was in me
Knew He was in London
Knew that God was London.

F. ? (six and a half years ago) 4540

My experience of the intervention of Jesus in my life will probably be very similar to countless other people's. With hindsight, I now know there were many pointers leading to this experience over a number of months.

It happened on a Passion Sunday. I felt extremely happy and joyful during the Sunday morning Eucharist and more so when the last hymn was changed from 'Glory be to Jesus' to 'When I Survey the Wondrous Cross', which has always been a favourite of mine, but the last line 'Demands my soul, my life, my all' began to mean something special to me. I went home and had lunch and after this sat at the table for a while. I have never been able to remember what I was doing. I might have been reading the paper, I just don't know. Suddenly I was filled with heat going right through me, feeling at first very frightened – I thought I was ill or going to die, I had never felt anything like it before – but in a split second I knew it was Jesus. I felt dazed, happy, full of joy.

I got through the day, got the tea and went to Evensong, hoping nobody would say anything trivial or they might break the spell, and I was enjoying this state far too much. Somebody did mention that it was a waste with so many lights on, but it just washed over me. I lived the next week in a semi-daze, but so happy. I couldn't understand why he (God) should want me at all, let alone make me so happy. I didn't know then the purpose. I sat dreamily looking into space as well as looking after the family, who I did share all this with, each one separately.

From that day it was like I was turned in the opposite direction. Nothing has been the same since; my eyes were opened; for the first time I could see. I am still a very ordinary wife and mother, but now I know the direction God wants for me. Until this time, although being a regular church-goer (I thought that this was all there was to it), I loved God but didn't really know him. I hadn't prayed regularly or read my Bible for years, but this first week after this experience I went and bought a Good News Testament and when I read it, it was like it was written for me.

This experience was a lovely glow and I felt God's presence like I had never thought was possible in this life. It stayed with me for days at a time, then would go and come back for shorter periods, but as I got to know him personally, so the original glow ceased, for now I know him as my Lord and my God.

I can honestly say this has transformed my whole life, and I thank God for his wonderful intervention in my life or perhaps just making me aware of him, as before I was blind, but now I see.

F. 60 (22)   4581

I had an experience when I was a young woman of 22, married and living with my husband in America. It was not an uneventful period of my life in general, but on the day of this experience I was under no particular stress and cannot recall having any emotion at all, or at least nothing approaching an 'emotional state'. It was about mid-morning. I came from the kitchen into the bedroom, sat at my dressing table, opened a drawer and began to do something quite ordinary, I can't remember what, when I was suddenly overwhelmed by the presence of God. I was absolutely astounded. I hadn't known there was a God at all. Having rejected the Roman Catholicism of my childhood while still in my teens, I was pretty much an atheist or agnostic and had no interest in religion. I had no such thoughts at the time, however. I was just shattered, shaken to the roots of my being. My initial reaction was that man wasn't supposed to know this and I must surely be going to die, and I stumbled over to the bed, got in and pulled the bedclothes up over me like a terrified child; it wasn't an attempt to escape — which would have been ridiculous, as God was manifestly within me — it was more a gesture to hold together, absorb the shock and not actually shatter. This was not a vision; no lights, no voices, but a much more immediate and definite kind of perception, as it involves recognition and not just apprehension of something or someone. In other words, this was not the apprehension of some being of incredible power and beauty and majesty who-must-be-God, this was 'our' God, awesome indeed in the majesty of His power, which I found personally to be absolutely breath-taking and could never have imagined, but 'ours' nevertheless in the sense of being non-alien, almost familiar in some way, the one whom on some level or another we have always known and instantly recognize even if we are seeing Him for the first time. God was entirely within me, not just some 'divine spark' or bit or whatever, but all of God; also, God was entirely without me, complete – I could lift my eyes to where He was – and this was one and the same God. This did not seem at all odd at the time, just natural, the way it was. Also, in case it needs saying, this was not an experience of some divine 'force' or emanation or other impersonal manifestation. God is a personal being to whom we can relate, not that I dared to address Him.

I told no one about the experience; it changed my life radically, but apparently in ways that were apparent only to me, as no one else appeared to notice any change in my behaviour. I did not return to church; nothing seemed more obvious to me at the time than that the Churches had no idea what they were playing with. Later, I trained as a psychologist, obtaining a PhD in clinical psychology and later worked as an Associate Professor. For the last few years I have been in private practice. Nothing in my professional training or experience has ever made me doubt the reality of what I have tried to describe to you. I am as convinced now, at age 60, as I was during those astonished days immediately following the experience. Indeed, I am still astonished sometimes. Why *should* there be a God? I can think of no convincing reasons. And a personal God at that! It all seems so unlikely! Then I am astonished all over again.

I have had some other experiences that might be called religious or spiritual, or perhaps just psychic, but some of these permit of more than one possible interpretation and none of them have the definiteness or importance of the experience I have related to you.

F. 35 (25) 4056

The experience occurred in the summer. I was 25 years old and living in a flat in London. I had been made redundant four months earlier, had no work, no money and had broken up with my current boyfriend when my job as a journalist finished. I was in a depressed frame of mind and living on a diet of brown rice and fruit for reasons of economy. At the time I was reading a great deal on alternative religions and had come across the work of Gurdjieff. I felt that part of my predicament was the lack of any spiritual purpose in my life. I was also doing about thirty minutes a day of yoga exercises.

One evening I was going to bed in a very low frame of mind and as I was undressing I 'prayed' very hard to be given a sign, was this delving into alternative religion merely an escape from reality or was it something real? This was a desperate and heartfelt prayer.

I then sat on my bed, the bedside light was on, my eyes were wide open. It then seemed as if the wall directly in front of me had disappeared, I was looking out into a vast night sky, the walls of the bedroom were still perfectly visible on either side. I could see the stars and a round blue ball, very beautiful, which was the Earth. A large, rounded man with a round, beaming face was sprawled across the sky holding this ball between his thumb and forefinger. I understood that this was God, who was taking the shape of this unlikely looking plump figure. Flashes of light hovered in groups at his extremities. I understood these were, or had been, human beings. The man's face was unbelievably restful and joyful, although he looked down sadly at the globe of the Earth, which seemed to be trailing clouds of smoke.

At this point I became frightened. I looked to the side, where I saw the walls of my room. I looked ahead of me and there was this night sky. The first pictures had dissolved; there was now a light which frightened me; I felt I would be engulfed. I screwed my eyes shut, shook my shoulders very hard and everything was back to normal. I do not know how long the experience was, two minutes or an hour.

For several days I was carried along on an immense tide of joy. The event made a deep impression on me, although I have only ever told three people about it.

Nine years later I met a woman who had a book in her house on an Indian religious leader, Sai Baba. There was a picture of a plump, round-faced man on the cover; it was the same figure who had appeared as 'God' in my vision.

M. 32 (3 or 5) 4123

When I was a child around 3 or 5 years old my uncle brought us for a drive in his car one afternoon. This drive took in a circle of the south side of the city. Half-way through the journey we approached a street. I observed a Catholic priest in full attire (ceremonial) celebrating the Holy Sacrifice of Mass on an altar hanging in midair outside this building (which I discovered lately was a nuns' convent). When I questioned this sight, it seemed no one with us in the car could see this or anything unusual. This experience I put to the back of my mind and I never thought any more about it. Until recently.

My mother was sitting at the fireside with most of the family and we were discussing the supernatural and the unexplained experiences one meets in one's lifetime when, to my amazement, my mother began describing an incident which happened to her when she was a little girl. The incident, she explained, was identical to my experience, only her experience or apparition was observed while on holiday as a child in the garden of an old cottage. This priest on the altar could only be seen by herself; the adults in her presence could not understand what she was talking about.

F. 54 (32) 446

At the age of 32 I had a mental breakdown, I suppose of schizophrenic type, for I had many electric shock treatments during the three years I spent in hospital.

At one time I reached utter despair and wept and prayed for mercy instinctively and without faith in reply. That night I stood with other patients in the grounds waiting to be let in to our ward. It was a very cold night with many stars. Suddenly someone stood beside me in a dusty brown robe and a voice said, 'Mad or sane, you are one of my sheep.'

I never spoke to anyone of this, but ever since it has been the pivot of my life. I realize that the form of the vision and the words I heard were the result of my education and cultural background but the voice, though closer than my own heartbeat, was entirely separate from me.

I have never had any form of mental trouble since. I am now quite alone except for friends, but I am perfectly happy, or perhaps content would be a better word.

F. 70 (25)   1131

You might be interested in an experience I had some years ago when I was in hospital. I cannot call it a religious experience though it gave me an assurance of survival after death. It certainly was an unusual experience.

I have worked on medical research problems all my life until I retired a few years ago.

In my mid-twenties I was in hospital with a severe injury to my spine and unable to walk. I was working as a lecturer. I was also engaged to be married. After being a week or two in hospital and not improving, I was feeling very depressed. One evening the sister came in and tried to cheer me up by saying they were going to pray for me in chapel that evening and I must not lose heart – there was always Lourdes. That night I was lying awake when my bedroom door was pushed open and a colleague came in from the school, an elderly man, named S, from the same department in which I worked. He was a brilliant scholar and a good friend of mine. He sat by my bed holding my hands, talking cheerfully and telling me to keep up my courage, for I was going to get well and would be back again at my work. He seemed to stay with me a long time and he looked just as he always did, in a black alpaca coat and very short hair, iron grey. I only realized he had gone when the night sister looked in. She said I looked better. I told her I had had such a nice visitor, who had cheered me wonderfully. She laughed at me and said, 'We don't allow visitors at this time of night. Do you know it is two o'clock?' This did not worry me. I knew he had come in somehow.

The next day my chief (the professor from the school) came to see me with the good news that a new expert on spinal troubles was coming to see me that afternoon. I thanked him and said I was feeling full of hope, as old S had been to see me last night and had restored some of my courage. I saw his face change. He rubbed the back of his head, a habit when he was worried, and said, 'I am sorry about this. We did not tell you, as we thought it would upset you, but old S died a fortnight ago.'

I did recover after about four months and returned to my job.

F. 52 (50) 4768

I was 50 years old when this occurred. At this time I was under severe mental stress with family and marital problems and difficulties in almost every direction, personal difficulties which I have had since 8 years of age. I was being ostracized by the small community in which I live. Also I realized that I was the cause of a great deal of unhappiness to other people, mainly through being immature and naïve to an almost unbelievable degree. I remember thinking I can't carry this load anymore. I struggled on another three months or so with more and yet more problems. I went to the church and sat alone weeping, I don't know how long for, when I became aware of a very, very gentle touch on my head, like a very low voltage. I stopped weeping, I couldn't understand it, when the same thing happened again. (Weeping not only for myself but those who were hurt by me in some way.)

The universe has always been incredible to me, but I had no really strong belief as to whether it was just an evolvement or was this designed by the creator, a supreme being. I have no doubts now and feel that no matter what I have done, this will be looked on with compassion, and I really try to live by his ways. I made a personal commitment in prayer.

My problems didn't end with this happening. There was, in fact, worse to come and it is only very slowly that I have realized the meaning of it and now 'my cup is full and runneth over'. I am almost frightened by the new way I now feel and I have surmounted quite a lot of my problems.

F. 81 (67)   **4315**

An old friend aged 94 was in hospital. She had had a heart attack some two months before, was admitted to hospital and was very cross when she found that the doctors had worked hard to save her life. She had been saying for some time before this that she really wanted to 'go to her mother' and be with her sister, who had died, at the age of 100, some time before. She was a sincerely religious person and said she had had enough of this world and wished to go home. She was sent 'home' after a few weeks in hospital – this home was now an old people's home, and she said she could not eat or drink, that she could not swallow.

She was readmitted to the hospital and would not co-operate with the staff in any way – she was no trouble, but refused food or drink and would not speak.

I visited her one afternoon. I'd not seen her for three weeks, as I hadn't been well myself. When I went to her bedside, a young nurse was trying to give her a feeding cup of tea. But she made no move to open her mouth and didn't respond to the nurse's coaxing. I asked the nurse if I could try; she gave me the feeding cup and went away. I bent over my old friend and said, 'It's M here.' To my utter amazement her face was transfigured – the only word to describe it – into that of a young girl, lovely skin, bright blue eyes and an enchanting smile; she looked 18 years old!! Slowly the vision faded and she became the very, very old lady again. She took the tea – but did not speak.

I left the hospital very shaken yet uplifted. I felt I'd seen the transfiguration and the resurrection – in a spiritual sense – and I still feel that. I am a very stable 81-year-old retired doctor – but feel it was a real experience – but quite unable to explain it.

M. 58 (30) 2496

On Sunday, 6 June, my parents went as usual to both morning and evening services at the chapel, but I did not accompany them. During the evening service I was out in the garden reading, and writing to friends. My mother was brought up by motorcar from the service unconscious and died a few hours later without having recovered consciousness. My father, then 78, was a man of exceptionally strong religious conviction and to a great extent overcame his deep sense of loss and grief by his belief that God had prepared the way for my mother's death and that she was ready to be received into the state of grace in God's surveillance some call Heaven. There were pointers to this in recent services she had attended during the last week of her life, which I could mention and recollect if necessary. We received, as usual at times of bereavement, letters of condolence, and one was of particular consolation to my father. Although I well remember I could not share in the deep conviction of the survival of my mother it contained, I was impressed by the following passage, which I entered in my journal:

She was as the Angels, who we are told are ministering Spirits. The great comfort we Christians have in death is that the love we have for one another is not broken by it, so that the very grave is full of hope. It is not only the memory of the past which strengthens us but the looking forward to that perfection to which our loved ones have gone.

I had grave doubts whether such a claim was justified by reality.

It was in this mood, and my belief that my mother had been buried for ever as an individual in the grave, that I set out on my five-mile bicycle ride to P the morning after her funeral. It was a fine June morning, with a still, blue sky. After I'd cycled for about two miles, to my right I heard the sound of a strong breeze coming towards me. I got off my cycle, at a point where I wouldn't normally dream of dismounting, and looked towards the brow of the wooded hill to my right. There was a sort of turbulence in the air, for which there appeared to be no apparent cause, and as the turbulence subsided, a bright radiance formed in that part of the air where the turbulence was subsiding and my mother's transfigured face (with her features readily recognizable) became visible to me. I could hear her voice filling my consciousness and the main purport of her words was to tell me that she had not been left for ever in the grave, that she was blissfully happy beyond all human belief and that I was to stay to accept responsibility for my father and not attempt in any way to communicate with her again during my lifetime. She said this as I experienced an almost overpowering urge to be drawn up into the radiance. She then withdrew and the radiance vanished, spiralling away, and the sky became its normal self, as I had always seen it before and have always seen it since. I made the following note in my journal at the time:

She broke through (i.e., the radiance) to fill my consciousness with the knowledge of the bliss she had attained to – the perfect unity that was possible beyond the grave – the joy of unity with God of which we here have but an inkling. To sorrow any more will only be a form of self-pity – she has shed her physical weariness – she is at one with Him in peace and love, and yet she still IS. That is the mystery.

This is the profoundest experience of my life and led to my taking up my responsibilities both at home and in relation to my chapel. I have taken my mother's advice as given me in the vision never to attempt to contact her again. It has left me with a quiet conviction of the truth of the Christian gospel and the claims of the Gospel.

F. 67 (43)   2563

One day I got a phone message to say that my elder son, who was at a public school in E, had been taken to hospital that morning with polio. As I lay across the kitchen table in complete anguish and despair, I distinctly felt my grandmother's hand laid on my shoulder and I had a feeling of complete serenity. My grandmother had died when I was 11. She was a very religious woman and I adored her. I just could not worry after this happening, and my son managed to throw off the germ before paralysis set in.

F. ? (?) 4104

Soon after my husband died – I cannot say how long – a few days or even hours – I saw him crossing a plank bridge which had been thrown across a stream.

The stream was in the midst of glorious country and there were fresh green bushes and trees everywhere. The plank was of old gnarled wood, not very wide and had evidently been utilized solely in order to get across the water. It was as simple as that.

His pace was slow but very sure. He never turned round, yet I felt that he was aware that I was following at a distance.

I could not see anything beyond his figure.

I had no doubt whatever that he would be lovingly received when he reached his destination.

F. ? (?) 4281

I would like to share with you a very simple and homely religious experience which gave me so much peace at the time and has remained with me.

It happened some time ago, a few months after my mother's death. My young brother visited me, just for the day. He was in very poor health and seldom did any work.

When he left, I gave him a blanket which had belonged to mother. As I closed the door and turned back into the hall, I felt a warm presence all around me. I saw no one, but I *knew* my mother was with me and she was glad. Instinctively, I cried, 'Mother!' Soon her warming presence left me. I smiled and a deep peace came upon me.

My brother died the following year at the age of 33 years.

F. 71 (many years ago) 2479

Many years ago I was very low in mind and body – for the first time I doubted God. As I lay propped up in bed I sent out a wordless plea for help. I became aware that there was a faint light in the room, which deepened until the room was full of a deep golden light and I knew I was in the presence of an immense power and love, and I felt the peace of God, which does indeed pass all understanding. I have never lost that inner peace.

M. 29 (19)   2723

The incident occurred when I was caught stealing a petty item that I rationalized wasn't worth buying. I tried to escape in fear of the embarrassment such an incident would cause to my parents. I ran, was caught and locked in a dark cellar while the police were summoned. I was horrified at the situation and in a half-frenzied state broke into tears, crying for God, someone, to help me, several times. I doubt that more than a few minutes passed like this, then I was silenced. Whether I actually heard a voice or just felt it, I can't remember, but that I was reassured and calmed there is no doubt in my mind. Since this incident I have again felt this reassurance on other occasions. I have come to feel that I am a part of something much bigger, a divine whole. Perhaps just a speck, but a part just the same.

F. 36 (34)   2049

About two years ago I had a very unhappy emotional experience, and that night I lay in bed, so filled with unhappiness and bitterness that I was unable to sleep.

I wanted to pray for comfort, but, adding to my bitterness was the knowledge that, as the whole thing had been my own fault, I didn't *deserve* to be comforted. Suddenly, two lines from the hymn 'Rock of Ages' flashed into my mind:

> Nothing in my hand I bring,
> Simply to Thy Cross I cling

and I knew, with absolute certainty, that I didn't *have* to 'deserve' comfort or forgiveness – they were just there for the asking. I understood, too, for the first time, fully, that this was the meaning of the 'grace' which is the theme of so many hymns. I knew that I was loved and forgiven, and in that moment all my grief and bitterness were melted away, and I went peacefully to sleep. I will never forget that moment of absolute peace and certainty.

F. 90 (10) 2495

At a very early age I was conscious of a feeling I can only describe as 'There is something else'. I did not know what this was, and did not associate it with religion. I know now that it was God speaking to me. Then when I said my little prayer, I wondered why we had to talk to Him like that. At last there came a time when I became very unhappy and felt I must be very wicked, and so begged God to forgive me and save me. (I must have been about 10 at that time – or even only 9.) At last, one night I wept and prayed, and several times got out of bed and pleaded with God to forgive me and help me. At long last I felt 'I must have it', for I could not sleep. And then the answer came, and I was just flooded with Joy and Peace. I cannot describe the wonder of it – words fail me. When I awoke the next morning it was nothing I had to recall, for the joy and peace had been with me all night – and the wonder and the joy remained with me for a long time. The world was a wonderful place – *everything* and *everybody* was beautiful, even the animals in the farmyard were beautiful.

F. 50 (28) 2565

My experience occurred when I was about 28, and there is not a day, I think, when at some time I do not call it to mind or that my life is not in some way affected by what happened. It changed me very much inwardly and I suppose this change has been manifested outwardly also. Surely it must have been, and is.

I had a quite serious breakdown after the birth of my first baby, and I was ill for a long time, though no one would have known from my outward appearance, I think. I got on with life normally as best I could but was beset by deep depression and bad fears, all caused by a chemical imbalance, so the doctor said! After my third child came I was again very low and really felt I couldn't go on any longer feeling *so* terrible, so afraid and so devastated – and so physically ill. This kind of mental stress takes a heavy physical toll also.

One night I felt so desperate that I just said in my mind 'God, you have just *got* to help me, no one seems to be able to.' Within seconds it seemed I felt aware of a great force of overwhelming love somewhere in the room, towards the foot of the bed, but I would say 'suspended' rather than on the ground. Anyway, that was how it seemed to me at the time. I seemed to have a great and complete inner awareness about the whole of the mystery of life. I felt aware of the uselessness of worry and anxiety, and the great love that surrounds every earthly creature. It was as though something was telling me that I could be well and didn't need to feel as I had for such a long time, that I was greatly and overwhelmingly loved by some force outside myself. I must stress here that I am and have always been exceedingly happily married and had no need to feel 'loved' in any earthly sense. I also would stress that this feeling came to me from somewhere 'outside' myself, definitely not self-created. This I feel most strongly and I would argue this against those who believe in any way to diminish it by saying it *is* self-created. If we in any way could for *ourselves* create this kind of feeling, then we wouldn't be able to cope with it on any sort of long-term basis; it is too extreme, too much to contain for very long. I felt aware of all the uselessness of the way we live and the great need to love one another and that this love is ours for the taking; we all have it within us.

It is hard, almost impossible to put this into words; for all the years since it happened to me I have tried to understand it. I find myself always thinking of whatever came to me as a 'comforter' (in the biblical sense as Christ said that after He was killed 'I will send you a comforter'). This to me was exactly what it was, but in terms no words can express.

I told my husband some time after. He noticed a change in me, I think. I wasn't *better*, no, that took ages, but I felt different and I knew that there was help at hand of a great and wonderful and lasting kind, help that would never get fed up or turn away and leave me alone to cope by myself, for, however good families are in this kind of mental distress, one *is* terribly alone.

M. 61 (48)

It was thirteen years ago. I was working for an electrical wholesaler.
A young lad, P, was working there with me. He was about 17 years
old then and very defiant; it may be it was for that very reason that
I took an especial interest in him.

The day was a black one and the rain started to fall about 10.00
a.m. During conversation P mentioned that he had a date for that
evening and that he hoped the rain would stop before then. I
informed him that I hoped so too, as I had no coat with me at the
time and would have to travel six miles to my own home. Suddenly
he spun round on me and said, 'You believe in God; ask Him to
stop the rain.' I explained to him that this would not be in
accordance with God's will, as it would be asking for that which
would please *me*, not to bring glory to the name of Jesus Christ. P
taunted me and pestered me the entire morning with expressions
such as, 'If God stopped the rain, *I* would believe in Him.' It
continued to pour and he kept insisting, 'If you prayed, He would
stop it,' to which I would repeatedly reply, 'It would not be in His
will.'

After giving the situation considerable thought, I made my way,
without the lad's knowledge, to an outbuilding where storage tanks
and general sundries were kept. The place was seldom used and
the dust was thick, but passing among the oddments and rubble I
reached the back of the building, where I immediately fell on my
knees in the dust and grime. Even now I still remember the basic
words of my prayer: 'O my Father God, open this young lad's eyes
and show him, yea there is a God, not only in Israel but in T, for
Jesus Christ's sake, Amen.'

The experience was miraculous. I heard no voice but something
within me told me the exact time the rain would cease, so that I
went with perfect assurance out of that old building. I would have
been willing, had I been a betting man (which I am not), to have
staked my life on it. The time was then around 12.15 p.m. and I
told P quite simply, 'The rain will stop at 5.15 p.m.' He exclaimed,
'You have asked God', but I would tell him nothing except the
assurance I had that at 5.15 p.m. the rain would cease.

All that afternoon he ran to and from the door, coming back with
the information, 'It is still raining', to which I would reply, 'It is not

'5.15 yet.' The sky was overcast and the rain fell in torrents all afternoon. At five o'clock it had not slackened at all. P continued to say to me, 'It's still pouring hard' and I kept repeating, '5.15'. Between five and ten past five there was a slight break in the clouds and a tiny patch of blue showed through. At exactly 5.15 the rain ceased. P's face was the colour of chalk and to me it was a joy to see. He said, absolutely amazed, 'Gee, there is a God!' and I said 'Halleluyah!'

I cannot truly say that the lad is devoted to Christ, but he strongly claims he believes and we refer to this experience from time to time. P himself would be quite willing to testify to the truth of this experience, I am sure, and although the sceptics might say it was merely a remarkable coincidence I know that the indwelling certainty of the time when the rain would stop was given to me from outside myself, directed to me from God through my faith in His son, the Lord Jesus Christ.

M. 54 (53)   2530

I had the privilege of being in Jerusalem last April. As I was waiting to go into the tomb where Jesus was buried, I was standing with my wife near a plaque or tomb on the floor, when I heard someone say they thought it was where Mary was buried. I was looking around the church of the Holy Sepulchre and thinking, 'Did all this really take place, was Jesus the Son of God, what proof has anyone?'

The floor under my feet seemed to explode, pain came up through my body – no, it wasn't pain, it was agony – all my body just ached. I felt sick and my stomach seemed to turn over, then my body seemed to burst into three parts. I saw a large figure, another smaller figure and then another as a bright shiny light; it only lasted about two seconds.

It was not until I returned to the Holy Sepulchre again that I found the spot where I had been standing was where Jesus had been taken down from the cross.

I had asked God for proof and that moment of agony seemed to answer my question.

M. 24 (21) 3088

On leaving school I followed my father's example and started training as a solicitor, and it was not until I was 21 that I asked Christ to control my life. At once I began to see myself unadorned and the world in a completely new light and saw in what direction I should be going.

Thus it was that I had my first experience of open Christian fellowship at the college I attended. In one Bible-study evening it was first suggested to me that one should pray *out loud* in one's own room!

So in these circumstances I afterwards got down to pray one morning in the quiet of my room and with a quite open and contented heart gave praise and thanks to the Lord for what He had done in changing my life, and for His goodness in entering the world and giving us hope.

Then, after some two or three minutes, I had this experience: a feeling took me over with such a swirling force of burning joy that I became terribly aware of the frailty of my body and I thought that the force would shatter my frame like a fragile eggshell, such heavings were within me. Yet it was also warm and comfortable and filled me with such a pure consciousness of the Truth that I have never had again. It was a vivid and utterly convincing vision. However, so strong was the force that after a few seconds I became terribly afraid that it would extinguish me; so it left me.

I got up and went off to work feeling awestruck but very blessed and wanting to let everybody know; but I didn't.

As to the effect that the experience has had on me:

1 It has defied any subsequent doubt.
2 It has led me to *know* that I am in the personal reach and power of God, and that He is manifestable and thus knowable in a most real sense.
3 It humbled me and showed me my own frailty and perishability.
4 I live conscious of Truth but can only *see* it fragments at a time, for my view is blinkered, distorted and at times quite clouded; but with this experience I *know* it exists in a perfect form.

I have never had as complete an experience again, not even at a pentecostal meeting that I attended some time afterwards. The wonderful thing about it is that it was utterly unexpected. It was a time when I wanted to *give* to the Lord in an unforced, unselfconscious way; I had *no idea* that I would get anything in return.

M. 43 (41)   639

I am a very run-of-the-mill post-Conciliar Roman Catholic: that is to say, rather bewildered, much less clear about what is right and wrong, much less formally devout than was the case before the Vatican Council. In October my 16-year-old son was diagnosed as suffering from aplastic anaemia. I was told that there was no way known of regenerating the bone marrow; that all that could be done was the sustaining of life by regular transfusions (in the event, every three weeks), and the protection of the body against other infections by massive doses of cortisone. I was told that it was a grave condition, and I discovered that it could prove fatal within two years.

In January, when things were at their worst, I began asking for specific things in prayer, and receiving them. From then on I had the experience of, as it were, praying him well, step by step. In June he received the final transfusion – I believe it was some thirty-eight pints of blood by that time. Last summer the haemoglobin stopped declining, then began to go up. The white corpuscles began to increase; then the platelets. The drugs were phased off. Total health and strength has returned. The doctors have said categorically: he had aplastic anaemia, nothing we were able to do has cured him, he is cured. In point of fact he is radiantly healthy, and we are all going out to Lourdes to say thanks at the end of this month. However, I know that the prayers of all sorts of people brought this about.

F. 59 (?)   2596

I was desperately ill. I had received my 'pre-op' shot, which had not taken very well, and I remember the long 'trundle' through the hospital corridors to the operating theatre. I remember also thinking that it was probably my last conscious living journey and I felt terribly frightened and alone.

At some moment in time during that 'journey' I became conscious of a person additional to the hospital staff walking quietly beside me. I recognized Him at once – like an old, familiar, trusted friend, and I tried to say to Him, 'My Lord, you need not have come yourself, one of your angels would have been good enough for me.' He did not speak, but somehow I knew that all was well and I felt no more fear or pain. I had a long uphill road to complete recovery (seventeen years ago) but I never doubted that I would 'make it'. I shall also never again fear to walk in the valley of the shadow of death because I know I shall not walk alone.

F. ? (?) 2562

Just a brief line to tell you of my experience of the nearness of God.

I had pains in my leg for a few days, and this particular night it was worse when I got to bed. After turning from side to side and not being able to get to sleep, I suddenly said, 'Oh, God, *make* my leg better' and immediately I felt the pain being drawn out, and my leg was quite better. This made me realize how near God is to us and that he does answer prayer.

F. ? (three years ago) 4426

I write, as I am not a person who can say that I have had frequent occasions of experiences like these and this happening was such a revelation that I shall never forget.

Five years ago I suffered an accident to my right leg and it was broken in many places. I had two operations and eventually after many months I received some physiotherapy. I was told by the consultant that he did not know how I would eventually walk. However, I have the personality that conquers most things and, with a lot of hard work, I eventually started to walk again.

However, since that time I always suffered pain in my leg, usually about three o'clock in the afternoon until the end of the day, and I thought that it would be something that I would have to grit my teeth and bear.

Three years ago I was on holiday in France and I was with four friends. It was in the afternoon and we had been walking a lot and I was longing to sit down and rest my painful leg. However, I walked into the cathedral at S and, as I was looking round at the statues of the saints, I suddenly felt a very intense warm feeling in my leg, just like someone was filling my leg up with warm liquid. All I know is the feeling was so very strong. I looked up at the statue facing me and it was of Saint Teresa. So overwhelmed at that moment, I remember emptying all the francs in my handbag and lighting the biggest candle I could see. Tears were streaming down my face and it was a few days before I could tell my friends what had happened.

Ever since that day I have not had any pain in my leg. Maybe only on two occasions have I had some slight pain. I feel something happened on that day.

F. 42 (32)   2526

This experience of 'being born again' happened about ten years ago.

Although I had what is called a nervous breakdown, I knew also that it was a breakdown in human relationships. Not being able to go to church, I continued in prayer at home and gradually all the things I had learned in Sunday school and church became clearer in meaning.

As I prayed, I realized I was being made to think, and that thought made me change personally – from being a self-conscious and uncertain person to one of peace and certainty. Becoming sensitive to the needs of others and less sensitive in myself, and not taking offence easily. I still marvel at the change which took place within me, and the gracious way in which it was carried out.

F. 71 (55)   4091

I was watching the news on TV. It was the Vietnam War. I saw children running from the bombs, screaming, wounded, with insides hanging out as they ran. I was so overcome with horror, and suddenly quite, quite certain there was *no* God. How *could* there be, to let this happen to innocent children? I jumped up in fury and ran from the room and, contrary to feeling sure there was *no* God, proceeded to tell Him just what I thought of Him. I looked at the sky and shook my fist and reviled Him for those suffering kids *and* that He'd let His own son die on the cross. I ranted and raved, and then cried out sneeringly, 'If *you* want *me* to *believe* in you, show me a sign.'

It came. Something like a tail end of a rocket, the sensation of 'twinkling' went through me and then my mind seemed devoid of all thought except GOD – the *awareness* and *reality* of God. My mind was filled with God. And then He chastened me. He called me a puny human, who'd had the effrontery to say what I did to the *Creator*. *I* was safe within my own four walls and if I thought *I* could do better, why didn't *I* get out to help people that came into my mind. When I came to myself, I was standing staring into space and feeling utterly ashamed of myself. I felt afterwards that because I had always believed in God, though vaguely, and because I had stormed at him for the sake of suffering on a human level, He *had* answered me, even though I needed chastening too.

The peculiar 'God in my head' feeling stayed with me a long time and, of course, has never left me entirely. He *is* with me. I was still very ignorant and thought I'd been converted, but some weeks later I was reading a booklet called, I think, *Four steps to Christ*.

As soon as I came to the invitation for accepting Jesus Christ as Saviour, inviting Him into one's heart and life and so on, I said, 'Oh! If this is what He wants us to do, I'll do it' and knelt down and gave my heart and life to Him there and then. But I had had *no idea* that this was what one did to become a Christian. I hadn't learned that in church.

But Jesus Christ has certainly changed my life. I was baptized a year later and since then have done things I'd never have dreamed of. My one regret is that I never knew Jesus Christ as Saviour years before.

I was 27, a confirmed atheist, cynical, worldly wise and super-
stitious. I think that was why I was finally persuaded to go to
church. New Year seemed like an auspicious time for church
visiting, even though this 'church' was a working men's hall turned
over for the evening.

The singing was very cheerful but when the preacher stood up, I
think I must have mentally switched off. He began to wind up his
sermon by saying, 'Is there anyone here who cannot go on ...'
Suddenly, I knew that that was me. I couldn't go on carrying all the
loneliness and fear and confusion that lodged continuously inside
me. Eagerly, I opened my mind to hear the preacher's next words:
'... without Jesus Christ'.

Oh no, that man in the long white dress, patting children on the
head! The one with arms for ever open wide, who allowed people
to hit his face, left and right; meek, mild. Was this how I was to
find peace, by swallowing my pride and accepting this symbol of
total self-effacement? Well, I could not go on as I was, that much I
knew, so if he was the only way, then it would have to be.

Please understand, up until this point I do not think I even
accepted that Jesus was an historical figure. I thought of him more
as an ideal, a fairy-tale figure. But what happened next changed my
understanding for ever.

Suddenly, the hall, the people, the chairs were blotted out; I
could see nothing but the Being in front of me: long white robe,
arms opened wide in welcome. Horrified, my mind said, 'It *looks*
like Jesus!' Not that he wasn't real enough, for I knew that if I just
stretched out my arm I could have touched him. There was no
question of his being real. For I could feel him, too, in tremendous
waves of power that seemed to throb out from his whole body. And
with that power came an awareness of absolute purity. I felt the
contrast of this between us very acutely. There was something so
immaculate about him, so all powerful, that I knew this could not
be the lowly Jesus I had once heard about as a toddler. I then
recalled that just a few days earlier I had sworn at the sound of his
name, and remembering it, I fell on to my knees in fear because I
knew that he had only to lift a little finger and I would instantly be
struck dead by the power that filled the air all around me.

But then, in my mind, I heard him answer me, gently and almost amused, 'Yes, I am Jesus. Won't you accept me?'

At this point I was overwhelmed at his humility! Would *I* accept *him*? By now, I could feel the love that he was directing at me, a pure, unqualified love of total acceptance. He knew about the swearing, just as I realized he knew about all the other ugly things in my life, but he just simply loved me! Even my mind could not answer such a priceless question but I guess he must have read 'Yes', for my whole being seemed to become filled with light and incredible joy. This Jesus, who *was* the Jesus of my childhood and yet now was something infinitely more, loved me totally and wanted to be a part of my life! Light and happiness poured in waves over me.

I do not remember much more of that evening. I remember seeing people smiling at me, shaking my hand. I remember hearing someone saying, 'You have started a wonderful new life tonight.' And thank God that has proved to be so. That was not the only occasion on which I was to be aware of that wonderful Presence. And as time passes I have come to realize more and more positively that that unqualified love that healed all my inner darkness is available for the whole world – if only a way can be found to channel it through.

MAIN EXPERIENCES

*

A number of people, when responding to the request for accounts, wrote of one experience and added that they had had many others. This one experience was a most important and most impressive one. It was often the first in that person's life and often happened in their youth. The other experiences were either linked or not to that one account.

In this type of account there is often a patterning detectable. The way in which the experiences happen, their background and their content make it possible for the person to recognize in them the guideposts for their lives.

The criterion for ordering the accounts in this chapter has been if there was a link with the main experience or not. There is no judgement made whether one type is better than the other; only the fact is stated, letting that speak in the way it is recorded in the accounts.

F. 67 (20) 4693

Many years ago I had what could only be described as an 'illuminating experience'. It has remained vividly in my memory ever since and has been repeated at various times, although the original experience seems to have been the most vivid and intense.

I had spent the night with a boy-friend – a man who was more sophisticated than I was at that time (I had a very narrow, moralistic upbringing and was educated at a convent, which I left at 16, to become a civil service clerk, which I hated). I was not 'in love' with this young man, but eager for experience and to learn more of the world of art, music, politics – all subjects which I was very interested in, but was too shy to follow up on my own. My family were completely without interest in these matters. Although brought up to be very strict in my religious obligations, I had cast these aside by the age of 18 or 19, and was trying to find my own way.

The morning after I had spent the night with my boy-friend was a clear, bright spring morning. His room was an attic in a shared flat. I opened the window and looked out, up the street. I was vividly aware of a brilliance, a light which surrounded every roof, chimney, distant tree-top. A kind of 'illumination' – a window opening a chink to show something, some state of 'being' – which existed outside of me, yet which I had been shown a glimpse for a few minutes. I said, quite without thinking, 'There's something there . . . there's something else, which I can't explain!'

I have had similar experiences from time to time – I can only describe them as an opening of a window, or the lifting of a corner of a curtain – they are always brief, not more than a flash, and the effect, or the glimpse they give of something more real than obvious reality, lasts for ever. Perhaps it is a feeling akin to religious experience? Or the highest reaches of art and music? I do not know. I am capable of being profoundly moved by music, painting, poetry, literature, plays . . . but these rare 'illuminations' go further than emotions.

I have always thought about them and, in a way, they have helped me to think more deeply about the 'otherness' of natural things, to evolve some sort of philosophy to try to sort out the mysteries of 'being' and 'not being'.

I have never discussed these matters with anyone else, not even my daughter, as they seem to be personal revelations, whose beauty and clarity would vanish if they had to be justified by explanations, or logic, or down-to-earth dismissals. Perhaps, after all, they *are* religious experiences?

F. 63 (33)   2505

One lovely sunny day I looked out of the window at a poplar tree in fresh green leaf. The wind sighed gently through the leaves, causing them to tremble. As I stood fascinated, I experienced the thought of *old*, that tree is old and I was identified with it. A sense of timelessness enveloped me, as though I had lived from the beginning.

I get this overwhelming feeling even when seeing trees and fronds on television. As though the aeons of time are all melted into Time itself.

F. ? (21)   2552

I am enclosing a copy of a letter which was written by my mother to her new husband. It is a description of a transcendental experience which she had when she was 21 years old. Apparently her husband is the only person she ever confided in. I did not know of the experience until I found the letter among her effects after both she and my stepfather were dead.

Although the family had always been vaguely Protestant, Mother's parents considered themselves free-thinkers and atheists. Darwin had proved the Bible was wrong and science was God.

Mother married at 18 and I was born when she was 19. When I was 6 months old, Mother contracted scarlet fever. Mother was in a coma for a month. While she was unconscious, her sister died. In that year Mother's father died. Soon after, her marriage broke up, leaving her with a child to raise, and no skills, in the worst years of the Depression. As she eloquently expresses in her letter, her whole world had fallen apart. This was the emotional setting for the experience she describes.

*

I take you back through the years to a night when I was 21 years old. At that time I walked in Gethsemane, as I have before told you. For me the days were raw, searing agony. Only in the secret stillness of the night could I find ease from the incomparable pain of living. In the dear, sweet covering of night I could stop the torrent of my feverish thoughts and be unmoving and alone, like a wounded animal. Then Something would steal softly and silently out of the dark, like a small breeze, and gently, tenderly, would wash through my heart; comforting, healing the day's hurt, closing the gaping wounds, washing away the dried blood. And as the soul within me was restored the unholy tension in my mind and body would release and I could sleep.

I accepted that Something-out-of-the-dark gratefully and without question. I didn't know what It was and I was too tired to ask. I knew It *was* and for the time being that was enough. Countless nights I lay, dumbly thankful, in that Something. I began to think of It as a sort of Presence and to develop a deep, affectionate feeling for It. Knowing It would be there at night made little breathing spots of comfort throughout the day when I thought of It.

You will remember I had been brought up to scoff at the idea of God and I had no feeling this was of Him. I had a vague idea It was some natural healing quality of the night, something like the ease found in hot water used for a sprain. But the idea was *very* vague, for, as I say, I just didn't question much. I remember wondering many times if other people knew about It, and It seemed to me to be part of some principle of nature too big and obscure for me to grasp. I wondered, too, why no one had ever written anything about It and why It was never discussed. Even sex, the Great Taboo, seemed to be less hidden than *This* in the world. I let these questions brush through my mind, but I didn't worry them at all.

And then one night a miracle happened. We were in the midst of a gorgeous golden autumn. The hour was late and I was alone. I lay in bed at an open window, watching the harvest moon through the trees as it spilled its silvered magic over the land. The air was cool and clean and utterly sweet with the fragrance of ripe grapes, the good, wet earth and fallen leaves. Lying still in the now-familiar 'Presence' I had found in the night, I felt myself responding more and more to the beauty-drenched fairyland outside. It was as though all the inherent goodness and loveliness in all nature had gathered itself into an unbearably exquisite essence and wave after wave of it was breaking over my consciousness, thundering silently into my being, rending me with its heavenly perfection. I could scarcely breathe with the thrilling, enthralling force of it; my pulse pounded madly and I felt myself bursting with the fierce desire to let this unearthly beauty pierce me, tear me, shatter me to bits. I longed with an infinite longing to rush to meet it, to melt forever into that ineffable loveliness and be no more except *in it*. With all the wild, joyous abandon of a heart tortured and long starved for love and beauty, my soul poured itself out in pure, impersonal love and adoration. As the sun shines because *it is light*, so at that moment I loved because *I was love*: it poured forth from me as pure and strong and good as sunlight, a warm, rising, mighty tide. And in the flood of that tide came the miracle.

In the twinkling of an eye, and with all the ease and simplicity and naturalness of the break of day, my consciousness was raised and expanded and powerfully suffused with the unspeakable glory of the full awareness of the fourth dimension of the mind, the 'Kingdom of the Heavens'. This was in no way a hypnotic or trance-like state: I continued functioning in, and was perfectly aware of, the three-dimensional world around me, but now I realized there was *much more to it than we could ordinarily apprehend*. There was a whole new, unexplored world lying just beyond this veil of our senses, which was so totally different from anything we knew as to completely defy accurate description.

The splendour of the experience was overwhelming, shattering me with such joy and awe that beside it all the joys ever experienced by the whole of the human race, added together since the beginning of time, in the three-dimensional consciousness were as the flicker of a match compared to the light and heat of the sun. Knowledge blazed through me, consuming the boundaries of my little, limited mind and readjusting my vision so that I saw the Truth of all things – that same Truth which He promised should one day set us free of all limitations, Truth undreamed of by our fumbling little minds. From the endless heights and depths of the utter Bliss which was my being, came a great, silent voice, speaking with the soft thunder of countless unseen raindrops falling on a mighty forest, saying, 'I am Alpha and Omega, the Beginning and the End – and the In Between!' And I was One, literally, with the Creator and His Creation; and all the mysteries of time and space and life and love were opened to me, and I saw and understood.

I saw the whole of mankind: that all are in the grip of evolutionary law, that all are pointed toward God, that *all experience*, good and bad, is for the sole purpose of developing man's awareness, and that one day every soul, however black, must inevitably reach its goal in the New Consciousness, the Kingdom of God. And the Voice echoed, 'And every knee shall bow to Him'.

And now I saw the meaning of *my* life and all its pain; and I was profoundly grateful for the very pain I had so lately deplored, for through it my sensibilities had been sharpened to such keenness that I could see and feel and *bear* the terrible beauty of this Cosmic Revelation. Now I knew my whole life had been a preparation for this one moment of supreme awareness and I was glad.

So, all these things having been eternally etched into my memory, and a holy seal being placed over my lips, I left that sacred height and returned to the valley of shadows in which men live, there to begin my search. The return to ordinary consciousness was almost too much. You cannot know, you cannot imagine the pain and shock, the horrible sense of *loss*, the awful *loneliness*. And all must be borne alone and in silence, for there is no one capable of understanding, advising, comforting; no other human being to look at you and say, 'I know, I understand.' Only God is left and sometimes He seems awfully far away.

The length of time I spent in the fourth-dimensional consciousness could in all probability be measured in minutes – perhaps even in seconds – or maybe the whole experience was instantaneous; I don't know. But this I do know: I came to realize that time, real time, is something entirely new and different from our three-dimensional conception of it. Space, too, has qualities undreamed of by our world. Individuality, personality, material forms, all are startlingly unlike our accepted view of them when seen in the light of expanded consciousness. Even our thoughts, our ambitions, sufferings, tribulations, temptations, victories, failures, the very desires of our hearts, are not what we deem them to be. And all the channels of expression used by man in our world, be they political, social, economic, religious, intellectual, sexual, creative and imaginative, all these are something else from what they appear to be to the three-dimensional mind.

I needs must *write* these words: I dare not *speak* them forth, lest they be eaten up by the mindless frenzy of this existence so 'filled with sound and fury – signifying nothing!'

M. ? (?)   4067

I would like to tell you of my own experience in this 'field', knowing that it would not be a subject to discuss normally, only with very close friends who from their own experiences, perhaps, in or out of meditation, would be inclined to believe.

Some years ago I awoke quite suddenly in the early hours, and in the half light I saw a cloaked and hooded figure standing by my bed. There was no aureola, nor any illumination whatsoever surrounding this figure; in fact, it appeared to be an ordinary person apart from the cloak and hood.

Then I had the feeling that my whole being was drawn in a great sense of Love out towards this figure; and when this Being raised an arm over my upper body (I do not know if it was part of the cloak that overshadowed me or, believe it or not, a wing) I had the sensation of being a part of a rushing, wind-like sound. Then my consciousness, my spiritual self, or atman, call it what you will, left my physical body and I felt myself rising into a light, a warmth, an overwhelming sense of Ultimate Being that increased as I rose upwards towards that cloaked arm or wing. It would be impossible to describe the nature or the brilliance of that Light as it increased in what must only have been milliseconds. Just when my ego, my spiritual being, was on the point of no return to the physical level of consciousness, I experienced the sensation of rising up against the 'wing' of the Being's arm, almost with a bump, and I returned most unwillingly, as if pulled by powerful elastic, back into the body on the bed.

From this time on, I have had a realization of the insignificance of the physical vehicle of consciousness when compared to the real spiritual self and its causal vehicle; a subject that at the time I knew nothing about and had no particular interest in.

The most difficult part of writing a letter such as this is knowing when to stop, for the danger is that, by telling too much, the reader's credence might balk and the entire subject matter be rejected. This would be a shame. Very shortly after this experience I was led to experiment with dowsing rod and pendulum (an ordinary chain, or even my dog's heavy chain leash serves equally well), and I found that I had been given what I believe to be a powerful facility in this field. Water, at the mundane dowsing level, I could find without any difficulty, although I have not capitalized, nor wished to, on this level. Shortly after this I discovered that by using certain movements of the dowsing chain for 'yes', 'no' or 'no comment', I have been able to communicate with the Being who visited me that night. Telepathetically the name Raphael was flooding my mind with a great persistency, until I was given to ask through the medium of the dowsing chain if it had been the Archangel Raphael who had given me that illuminating and life-changing experience. The answer was a very emphatic yes. I have had a very great deal of proof since then, by working with this Being of the hierarchy, that it was indeed him.

F. 50 (43)   4384

At that time I gave very little, if any, thought to spiritual matters, being busy bringing up a family. I suppose I would have been classed as an agnostic. The death of my mother, however, made me begin to search for some deeper meaning to life. I remember passing the library in the town I was living in at the time and felt compelled, almost pushed, in. I had never been a member of a library and read very little. I joined there and then and walked straight to the section on philosophy/comparative religions, etc. I became an avid reader of books on the incarnation, karma and out-of-body experiences. I spent all my spare time reading and learning to meditate. It was at this time that I had my experience.

I was sitting in the dentist's chair waiting for the dentist to examine my teeth. I was alone and looking out of the window. It was a dull, overcast day, but suddenly the sun came out – golden and glorious. This was not the physical sun, but a wonderful golden light. With it came a feeling of great joy, peace and well-being. I was so full of love for all things that I felt my heart would burst, and such a feeling of Unity. I was aware of a hand holding the whole world in its care – regardless of race, colour or creed – this was God caring for all his children. I felt that had I been at home I could have prolonged it, but it faded and the dentist came in and life went on, but never quite the same after. I couldn't think what had happened to me or why it should have happened to me, but it has been my anchor ever since. It loses so much in the telling, of course. I have never doubted since that day that there is a God and that he is a God of Love. This is not to say that my search has ended, it is still going on, but I feel that it was given as a gift to encourage me to keep on.

F. 14 (13)   4560

I have had an experience. This happened about a year ago. It was sometime around 12.30 a.m.–1.00 a.m. I was just falling asleep for the second time when I felt that there was something in the room. I felt totally at peace with the whole world. I felt as if nothing could hurt anything and that only good things could happen. It's difficult to explain. I saw everything in a new light. All the time I felt like this I could see a sort of face. All the time it was smiling but it kept changing; one minute it was bearded, the next clean-shaven, the next a woman, etc. I could feel that it was good. I could see my bedroom roof through it and it was floating near the ceiling to my left and near the foot of my bed. I wasn't really there but it was! I think it was with me for five, maybe ten, minutes and when it left I said aloud 'Please don't go'. I still loved the world and it felt like it loved me, but it was a sad love because the thing wasn't there any more.

Since then I've always felt there is something with me, listening to me and my thoughts. Watching and waiting. I can feel it now looking over my shoulder as I write this, but it's a different feeling. It still loves me but not like before, it's less apparent. It loves me just as much as it did before, but differently. It may all be my imagination but I don't think so.

F. ? (?) **657**

The event of which I write took place on the afternoon of 13 September at four minutes after four o'clock. I was well, full of high spirits after being able to be of witness to two friends who had had vexing problems. The feeling of elation at helping these two was uppermost – there was no sadness or grief in my mind, only contentment and joy. I was waiting in my studio (I was a busy piano teacher at the time) and the hour for my first pupil to arrive was drawing near. At the piano I was rather killing time by playing over some of my teaching material when this never to be forgotten event took place.

All at once I felt someone near me, a Presence entered this little room, of which I became immediately conscious. This feeling or second sense is a common one and could be very frightening, but I was not afraid or alarmed. I saw in my mind our Blessed Saviour and the picture of Him has never left me.

He was standing there visible only to my inward eye. His shoulder and face were turned from me, but His arms were outstretched. His long brown hair hung down to His shoulders. He wore a robe, with cloak or drape round His shoulders; the colour I could not say.

Dazed, I knelt by the nearest chair and here is the physical phenomenon that has recurred many times since. Into my heart there came a great warmth. The only way I can describe it is in the words of the disciples on their way to Emmaus, 'our hearts burned within us'. My hands, raised in prayer, also glowed from tips to wrist with a blessed warmth and heat never before experienced. This lasted for many minutes, perhaps ten, twelve, or it may have been longer. I was too dazed, humbled, elated to record it. Only as the days and months have passed have I appreciated the magnitude of this experience and marvelled.

Time without number since that time, as I have prayed, been inspired by some sermon, some beautiful act or scene, I have found that warmth coming back into my heart.

M. ? (?)   1637

After I felt the call of God to trust Him for everything I was in the
RAF as an aircraft mechanic. After a short time I was posted to the
Far East and during the trouble we were required to keep up a
fighter umbrella. This meant I had to decide which aircraft to
service first and which had to be left to the last. Imagine a line of
fighters as one taxies to the far end and one to the other. We were
short staffed in my trade. I trusted God to guide me to the right
plane and in my mind came a quiet voice. I obeyed the code letters
and raced to that aircraft. As I did, my heart was filled with joy to
the brim. After the trouble was over I worked it out to 360 aircraft
checked without the mistake of servicing the wrong one. I can write
a small book on how God has guided me and also fill it with
everyday happenings which I know come from our Maker, not the
subconscious.

M. ? (25)   4107

In my early years I had contact with the Church through Sunday
school, singing in a choir and later church going, though my
parents were not regular church-goers. I had some contact with a
Christian group and church when I was at university. The period
that I spent in the army was unsettling; I drifted away from the
Church and I suppose that I would have classed myself as an
agnostic as far as belief in God and Christ was concerned.

After demobilization and resumption of university career, I
continued the search for a satisfying philosophy and faith. I met
and talked to several people who probably influenced me without
my knowing it, but the turning point came at·the time when I
became emotionally involved with a female student who had
recently become a Christian and to whom this new experience
meant a very great deal.

During this emotional upheaval I returned to my digs one
evening and as I sat resting after the evening meal on my own in
my room I saw a vision very clearly of myself wearing a clerical
collar and in a pulpit in the act of preaching. As the vision faded I
was rather disturbed at such an unusual and unexpected event,

though, as I have explained, the incident took place when I was already in a charged emotional state. I went on to play badminton to try to take my mind off what I could not understand.

Shortly after, I borrowed a new translation of the Bible from the library and as I was reading a passage from it one night I felt for the first time in my life that God was speaking to me in the words that I was reading.

Following closely after I had further mystical/spiritual experiences which made me strongly aware of the presence of God, once at an uncle's wedding where I was best man and also during Holy Communion services. It would be impossible to describe these experiences in words but they were connected with, and deepened, the setting where they occurred.

At one stage I felt consciously that a kind of integration was taking place within me and that, as it were, I was being made to face in a particular direction.

At the same time as this vision occurred, I forgot to mention that I was made aware that I should go far afield with the message.

At Epiphany (I was immediately back in church), which followed soon afterwards, the conviction that I should go overseas was strongly reinforced by the service and the sermon.

Among the changes that took place in my life the greatest was the confidence I now felt to face new challenges, though I was well aware that I was being given help from outside to meet them also.

I was seconded from my teaching post for a year to train for the ministry. I was ordained deacon and served as a part-time curate as well as returning to my teaching post. I was ordained priest and went to South India to lecture in English and to be the chaplain to the church of South India students. In this way the vision came true.

What I consider particularly remarkable is that I had never intended to enter the ministry and certainly never thought that I should return to India (where I spent nine months during my time in the army) as a missionary. I now felt that my life had far greater purpose and meaning, and looking for guidance has remained a constant attitude.

When I was 17 years old I joined a religious organization called the Rastafarians, who preach that the 'truth' is written in the Bible and that it is up to the seeker to read and find it for themselves. I used to read my Bible a chapter a day and through this and prayer I developed my initial zeal for God. However, after a couple of years I left the organization and I decided that I wouldn't join another organization or Church until I found the 'right' one. For a couple of years I just led an ordinary life, not attending any kind of religious service and not even reading the Bible any more. Then I met a girl who was a member of an organization called The Divine Light Mission, who invited me to go along to one of the meetings and to 'experience' Guru Marah (I don't know the spelling).

That is the night that it all began. I went along to the meeting with a completely open mind and, to be honest, it didn't impress me very much. Most of the followers seemed dazed (or hypnotized) and although I thought the whole experience rather weird, I had no desire whatsoever to jump on the bandwagon. Anyway, when I got home and got into bed and closed my eyes the strangest thing happened. The Guru's face was in my mind so clearly that it was like looking at a technicolour photograph and then what happened next I can only describe as a 'vision'. I would like to point out at this point that I am not a hysterical type of person and usually have my feet firmly planted on the ground. When I closed my eyes then, my mind seemed to be taken over by what I can only think is my subconscious self, as it was all happening to me and it was a similar experience to watching a film whereby I was an objective viewer. I could hear my 'self' asking questions and then the answers were being displayed to me in brilliant technicolour in the form of a silent movie. If I came to a part which I didn't understand, it would immediately stop in action until I comprehended (which was perhaps a matter of seconds). Everything I saw was matters pertaining to my own life, which have since proved to be perfectly accurate. I don't know how long the 'vision' went on for, because I just wasn't aware of time, but it seemed like perhaps half an hour. I would like to stress also that I was *not* asleep and I kept opening my eyes to prove it to myself. When it finally ended, which it did just as suddenly as it started, I was in a state of amazement. It moved me very much but confused me even more, so I prayed to God and begged him to reveal the truth to me. I was wondering if this experience meant that the Divine Light Mission was the 'way' but not accepting it as it was because it was a pure 'mind' experience and not really heartfelt. I prayed to God and asked him to show me this experience for what it was because there was nobody else I could talk to about it. (My friends would think that I was crazy.)

When I woke up the following morning I can only describe myself as a totally different person.

From the second I got out of bed I felt the presence of what I know to be Jesus Christ with me. I suppose people call it being reborn. I can only describe it as the happiest, most fulfilling experience in my life. I have had some very happy times and have had a wonderful love affair with a man I would have sacrificed heaven and earth to be with, but this surpassed any feeling I have ever known and I know that nothing else could come near it; it was like I was in a state of 'perfect love' and all personal things became secondary to the overwhelming love that I felt for all living things. It was at this point that I actually felt holy.

My friends noticed the change in me, and the girl I was staying with actually threatened to throw me out because she said that she was scared of me because I'd changed so much. I suppose the biblical description of my state of being at that time would be that 'the holy spirit was upon me'.

This state of being was strong at first but after a few weeks it waned due to my own self-doubt of whether or not I could live this life dedicated to such a selfless cause.

Since then I have yo-yo'd between one thing and another and haven't experienced anything nearly so profound, but my faith in God is now like a rock.

F. 38 (33)   2011

I can say that God is real to me. I know Him. I had a personal experience of the Lord Jesus Christ at my conversion at the age of 33. It was the most wonderful feeling of happiness I have ever known. I prayed to Jesus alone and it was after this, when lying in bed, I had this overwhelming feeling of happiness. It was all around my heart. I knew myself forgiven and loved.

I had given up going to church although I was brought up Church of England. God had never been real to me and I had given up praying.

I found God through taking a course of *Guide to Faith* letters. In these they said God could become one's greatest friend and could be known. How I wanted that.

I couldn't live without Him now. I always go to church on Sundays. The most wonderful thing is having a friend one can tell everything to.

F. ? (?)   4350

The following is an account of the first experience I ever had. I have had others since then but the first one was the most concrete in that it came through my sense of hearing.

About two months after my father died I was taken ill with a type of flu. I was in bed and alone in the house. I was very frightened or I suppose it would be more accurate to say I had an attack of nerves. As night came on I became really terrified of being awake and sick and alone. I had my father's rosary beads in my hands and I was trying to pray. I heard a voice saying 'my child'. This was said in a 'loud' whisper and was outside myself. I perceived it through my auditory sense. At the time I thought it was my father speaking to me. I was immediately filled with great peace and lost all my fear and agitation. I was then able to go to sleep.

Perhaps God spoke to me or perhaps it was my father. I am more inclined to think it was God. Since then God has twice spoken to me by an 'interior' voice inside myself – almost like a thought coming into my mind. I only tell you that to emphasize that on the first occasion it was a definite voice coming from without.

F. 70 (14) 3006

When I was 14 years of age one day I had a shock. When I recovered, I could not stand alone. I did not walk for over twelve months. My parents were only poor but they saved enough money to get a specialist and then another one (one got no help those days). Both of them said it was TB and I would never walk again. We all gave it up, but a few months after, I dreamt I could walk. The room seemed full of light. I felt some power within me I could not understand, so the morning after, I asked father if he would help. He had no hope, but he did help me. We went on day after day for about two months. At night I sometimes felt hopeless, but the day after, I always felt I had contacted God the Spirit mentally. I did not beg and pray for help; I just accepted that power within. I kept saying to myself, 'God the Father dwells within me. He'll fulfill my need.' And he did. I could walk, I could run.

My husband had a nervous breakdown. It was a long time before he would listen to me. Then I said, 'Do it inside yourself for a few days and don't tell me.' He did then. Later, he was a lot better. He said, 'Yes, the power is there if we accept it.' We have used this power over the years. We have had a lot of trouble and hard times but the power is always there and it is inside everybody waiting to be used. After all, our Lord said, 'The Kingdom of God is within you', so we are all born to be kings many times.

Now my husband and I feel that peace that passes understanding though times are hard.

F. 67 (?) 2498

After losing my husband, some years ago, I suffered a severe nervous breakdown, which reduced me to a shadow. However, being a Christian, I prayed and prayed to God continually for healing of this terrible breakdown, and after weeks and weeks of prayer, I awoke early one morning and heard a soft voice say 'I will not strike thee, I will heal thee.' I got out of bed thinking one of my children had spoken to me, but they were all fast asleep in bed. I continued to improve slowly, but still had the ague bouts (trembling), which troubled me very much. I got up as usual, early morning, and prayed earnestly to God for complete healing of these bouts; in fact, I touched the hem of His garment in prayer and tears, and immediately a stillness came over me and I never had another. Praise God.

I have since had remarkable experiences, which would fill a writing pad. One has to have an experience and the assurance in one's heart to believe in the Lord Jesus Christ and I have got just that. I trust this experience will convince someone that we serve a living Saviour.

?F. ?M. 69 (25)   2726

I was spending two weeks holiday with family friends in Switzerland. The son and his young bride returned to the home from their honeymoon while I was there and his wife, R, developed a poisoned hand. There were no antibiotics at that time and she became critically ill and was being nursed at home by nurses. On the third day the specialist decided she should be admitted to hospital for the possible removal of the arm. She was in great agony and I could not bear to hear her cries and atmosphere in the house and decided to go for a walk on to the side of the mountain, the other side of the town.

It is quite beyond my powers to describe my experience on that mountainside – only that I prayed for help for R and that I had to return at once and go to her bedside.

I do not remember the walk back, but they told me I walked into the bedroom and ordered the nurses and husband and mother-in-law to leave the room. They did so without question. I sat down beside R and laid my hand on her arm (which was supported by cushions). She was soon asleep and remained so for that day and the night. I stayed in that position not needing sleep or nourishment. When she awoke at noon the next day, the swelling in the arm had gone, there was no pain and the healing was complete by the next day.

After a night's sleep and food I had to return to England.

Needless to say, the family were overwhelmed and the nurses and I received letters of gratitude, but I never felt this a personal achievement – only very humble at being used – so never kept the letters.

The intense joy of my experience remained with me on my journey home; I seemed to be living on a cloud.

Many people have received help since then from the same source, but for me there can never be quite the same spiritual experience as on that first occasion on that mountainside.

M. 51 (?)   4607

I am married, with a 12-year-old daughter. About five years ago I became interested – because of my wife's severe illness – in what are known as alternative or complementary therapies. My wife received acupuncture treatment and what is now known as spiritual healing. Our attitude to these treatments was purely practical: there was a limit to the efficacy of orthodox medical treatment, her spastic condition was worsening to the extent that she could no longer walk unaided. She received considerable benefit, over a period of time, from both these therapies. As a result of this, we both became intensely interested in what has now become known as the holistic approach to the treatment of illness.

Some two years ago I found that I was able to help her myself by the 'laying on of hands', i.e., spiritual healing. This was completely unexpected on my part and happened one evening at her request. She was in pain and asked me to place my hands on the affected part. This relieved the pain. But this action had a temporary adverse effect on me. I found that I had a strong feeling in my hands of what can only be described as 'pins and needles'; this lasted continuously for a week, even disturbing my sleep. Eventually, I was able to 'control' this feeling by telling my body to 'switch it off', so reaching the stage where, as one pushed a light switch, it was brought into use.

Naturally, I was intrigued as to what this healing energy was and, of course, the more I researched, the more I found that it was quite common: many religiously based movements – such as the spiritualists – had practised this for many years.

I have worked with established spiritual healers for two years or so, but my attitude is still practical: healing works; I am a useful channel for whatever the healing energy is.

Even so, it would not be reasonable to suppose that after my experience I would not be interested in what is called extrasensory perception; indeed, I have always had a keen interest in religious thoughts and beliefs, even though I do not belong to an established religious organization, except the Unitarians.

But this background, I feel, is necessary for the 'spiritual' experience that happened about six months ago. The conditions were as follows:

We were holding our regular healing meeting in our home, which is held on the same day, each week, from the same time. The procedure is as follows: the person receiving healing sits down comfortably, closes his or her eyes and, hopefully, allows the healing energies to come through. While this is taking place two or three people are sat quietly in the room, meditating and praying. There are no distractions in the room, except sometimes low suitable background music. There is no harsh lighting; it is dim, but not dark. The whole healing procedure, the laying on of hands, lasts about fifteen minutes.

That evening I was the 'duty healer', and the patient was a young woman who, I knew, was a healer of long experience. She is also a strongly intuitive person, religious in a broad sense, and has certain psychic faculties. After placing my hands on her shoulders, I felt a great receptivity from her (I should add that I always close my eyes when I am healing). From then on, until I finished the healing work, I experienced what I can only describe as a feeling of elation, of oneness with everybody in the room; a sensation of sheer 'goodness' permeated us both that I had never felt before. And even though, as I have stated, my eyes were closed I could 'see' the most beautiful white light.

At no time did I feel as if I was 'taken over'; I was in complete control of both my mental and physical faculties. The only word I can think of to describe the complete experience is joy. But I must stress that this was in no way a sensuous experience – it was purely spiritual.

The sensation lasted for the length of the healing, and all in the room felt the effects for some time afterwards. We did not discuss it at any length; there really did not seem much point.

I have not had a repetition of this. Many of the people who have received healing have felt deep reactions since, but not to the level of which I have just described.

F. ? (twelve years ago)   2604

Twelve years ago my husband died after a most distressing illness and many months of growing paralysis. Neighbours and friends were so kind, but somehow I seemed numb inside and couldn't forgive myself for not being with him at the end, and I slept badly.

However, the third night after, came my most wonderful dream – or, rather, I'm sure it was a vision, as ordinary dreams are so soon forgotten. I dreamt I was in a large field and crowds of folks were coming towards and passing me, and all looking ahead (and I vividly remember one man with a beard who looked at me so kindly), but amongst them I was searching only for one face, my dear husband. Finally, in despair I gave up and went home, and on opening the door found him sitting in his favourite armchair, and in joy I cried 'Oh, you're home!' and went to him, and I felt the gentle pressure as he put his arm round me (he was so weak).

How can I describe the wonder and glory on his face? The memory makes my heart beat so fast even as I write after all this time. His face was so young and smooth, and a wonderful radiance all about him – even his eyelashes seemed tipped with sparkles of gold. He gave me the sweetest smile, which filled me with the strangest sense of happiness, even elation, and then he turned and resumed the same attitude as when he died.

I awoke sobbing, but they were tears of happiness – he had come back to comfort me and I knew he was surely 'home' with joy and at peace with his Lord, who had most surely made His face to shine upon him.

Since then, both dear parents and several loved ones have passed on and, apart from a sense of deep loss, I have never really grieved, and even rejoiced knowing they were at peace in God's keeping.

So many times I have felt that my husband's spirit was with me, that he knew all that was happening, and several times when clearing up his affairs I was aware of a strong sense of guidance. I am sure I have received new strength and courage that I never possessed before. I cannot imagine how folks can cope with life without some faith and the loving power of God.

F. ? (?)　　　　　　　　　　　　　　　　　　　　4233

I was staying in Ireland in a cottage by the sea, with a beach, sand dunes and mountains. Walking through the dunes to call the family home from their fishing in the river, I came to the hollow I had walked through many times. This time I was halted by a voice saying clearly 'Take off your shoes, the ground on which you stand is holy ground.' I had no shoes on, but I was compelled on to my knees and then into a crouch so that I was as close as I could be to the ground. Then a tremendous silence came around me; I almost felt it touched me, I was enclosed in it. Yet I could hear the insects, bees, beetles, ants, etc. in the small flowers in the short grass, and I was one with them, creatures and flowers. I could hear the sheep and the breakers beyond on the beach, and I was one with them and the sea. Rivers, and for some reason the Victoria Falls (which I have never seen), came into my mind, and I was one with all waterfalls, all trees, all living things everywhere. A farmer's wife in the valley had just had a baby and I was one with them, and the old woman on the mountain who was dying and her relatives who were with her before they left for America, and I was one with them. Not only 'one with', somehow I was them. Then I thought God is here, with me and in me, the Creator, and for that moment I was one with and in God.

I don't know how long this lasted. I never got to the river. I don't know where I went or what I thought and it was much later when I arrived back at the cottage. I knew I had experienced something tremendous. But from that time my whole spiritual outlook(?) understanding(?) changed – I had been given new insights.

This happened a long time ago but will always remain clear with me. I have never had anything quite like that again, but at other times I have been 'arrested' and enclosed in the same silence. Later I have found I have learnt something, but always the 'somethings' have arisen from the silence.

Some years later the ending of one of Kenneth Boulding's sonnets confirmed some of my thought since that time:

> But something that moves among the stars
> And holds the cosmos in a web of law,
> Moves too in me . . . (?)[sic]
> A quick thaw of soul that liquidates the ancient bars
> As I, a member of creation, sing
> The burning oneness binding everything.

F. ? (24)   4136

I was pushing my bicycle up a small hill when I was suddenly 'arrested'. All I was conscious of was a swirling mass of white light around my chest and head.

I had just been to a Toc H meeting and had heard a moving talk on Poperinghe, followed by a short service.

I had an overwhelming feeling of cleansing and uplift and was left in a state of excited serenity and friendliness to everyone.

As an infant I was not christened but have always maintained that was my baptism by the Spirit – or Inner Light, as the Society of Friends say.

I have also had three experiences of 'seeing' people who have passed over.

F. 70 (43)   4071

It is not easy to select what incidents to relate of my own experiences. I will 'open up' and trust my guidance.

When a child, I 'received' two clear messages together. One was that 'Love was the answer to the whole world's problems.' The other, that 'The world is upside down.'

I was too young to understand either message but both stayed with me always. The first one I intuitively 'knew'. The second one I believed but without understanding. It took decades to be clarified.

I will skip a few years. My son was near death with active TB. The lead-in to the experience was miraculous, but too lengthy to relate. I 'opened up', for the first time in my life, totally emptied of self, and concentrated on my son's lung 'whole' (it had a large hole in it). Until that moment I had no conscious awareness whatever of the world of spirit or of other dimensions.

Then I had a profound experience. I knew that a veil was lifted. I was as God. I was everywhere and everything. The only two things I now remember being was a tree and a squirrel. I thought how odd it was that anyone had difficulty accepting that God *was* everywhere and everything. *I* was, and it seemed so natural and obvious. Also I saw millions of jigsaw pieces all floating into their correct position. All was well. All was completed. As I know now that it is; but within our Earth concept of time and space, we still have the working through of it to accomplish.

I have no idea how long this state of heightened consciousness lasted, but at some time during it I made the commitment 'Thy will (not mine) be done'. Because of my state, it was obviously my Higher Self that made the commitment. It was years before my conscious self could repeat it with integrity.

I was thrown into the deep end, not understanding what it was all about, but I was immediately given guidance in writing, where to start off so that I could begin at A, after experiencing Z.

From then on I have been guided every step of the way, as everyone is after commitment. Again, as with most people on the path, those steps took me into great darkness and hazardous journeys. Many times I had difficulty in believing in the light at the end of the tunnel, but I learned to have total trust in the process.

F. 19 (?)   4217

Quite often I find I have a feeling of not being myself. I seem to be looking out of myself. I feel trapped inside my body and *know* I am somehow waiting. Whatever I am doing at the time seems silly; for instance, putting a record on a turntable. My arm and the objects appear to me to be the same. Just objects. My body feels unnecessary, but necessary up to a point.

When I look at the stars in the night time, I feel outwardly insignificant but inwardly vast. I experience the most beautiful feeling of serenity. I don't feel like a body any more. I feel I am the stars, the wind, the trees, etc. Everything seems to be all right and I know somewhere inside is everything and everybody.

I hope this account is not the only one of its kind. I feel sure everybody should feel this somewhere at some time.

I never believed in 'God' before I had these feelings. I still don't believe in the concept of 'God' as a person or a leader. I think 'God' is a definition of the feelings in everyone that survives after death (the soul if you like). In short, together, all of us inside, we are 'God'. Therefore the phrase 'God is Love' is more appropriate than people may think.

I am not a member of a religious cult but I am what the older generation would call a punk rocker (though only mildly). This, however, is just a fashion trend, 'look', not a whole new philosophy, as older people seem to think and worry about.

However, I have considered turning to the Wicca religion – the only one that appears to see God as everything, nature, the universe, etc. I cannot agree with any religion that sees God as one person. But after my 'realization of soul' experience, I realized you don't have to go anywhere to be with any other people to 'worship', you can just be peaceful, thankful and wondrously happy in yourself.

F. 43 (36)   2772

Seven years ago last June my husband left our house fit and well after eating a hearty meal. Three hours later he was dead. He was just 38 years old. I had two children, aged 5 and 6 years old, and felt absolutely shattered. I just couldn't believe he was dead, and kept expecting him to walk into our home as usual.

He died on a Wednesday evening. On the Saturday my brother took me to the Chapel of Rest to see his body. This was the moment of truth and it hit me right between the eyes.

That night I broke my heart. The sight of him in the coffin was more than I could bear. I was lying in bed, as low in spirit and mind as I have ever been. Suddenly in the corner of the bedroom I saw him. He wasn't life size, but in perspective somehow. He was standing, leaning casually on his coffin as if it was an ordinary piece of furniture. The lid was off and stood propped against the coffin. He was smiling at me in a sort of reproving way and saying over and over again, 'Where is your faith, Z, where is your faith?' I would say I saw this for about one minute, but it's hard to judge. It wasn't a ghost – to me, it was a 'heavenly vision' sent to help me over that time.

When he was alive, those were always his words to me in troublesome times during our marriage.

Needless to say, through this 'vision' and God's love and help I was able to live each day as it came.

I must repeat; I was not sleeping nor dreaming, I had no sleeping tablets, I was fully *awake*.

The way I see it is this: although my belief in God was strong, at that particular moment my faith was weak. Too weak to see beyond the coffin and the grave, too weak to believe in the resurrection of the dead and the 'many mansions' that Jesus has promised us.

There have been many incidents in my life of God's guiding hand, but never one as clear as this.

M. ? (?)   4248

My life since 1935 has been studded with words that can only be ascribed to Almighty God and addressed to a very ordinary man. To give you these incidents would require a volume. Perhaps you will be able to draw valid conclusions from some examples.

In 1935, while facing an acute personal crisis, I rejected angrily advice offered by the local vicar. 'Unless you are prepared to do the Will of God,' he said, 'everything you do will turn to dust and ashes.' How can one know the will of God? Days later as I sat in front of the fire, without any intention I did something I had never done in my life before; I leapt out of the chair on to my knees and cried aloud without realizing what I was saying: 'O God, whatever You will, that will I do.' He did not speak to me but He acted in a way I could not have imagined possible. I received an invitation to take up a most important appointment; I accepted it and the result was a move hundreds of miles away and a wholly reunited family.

It is now exactly fifty years since that initial adventure. In all the years that followed I have never lost the sense of His direction, holding me to that original commitment. Doubts and failure have constantly assailed me but always, without exception, when turning towards that enduring, invisible, inaudible Presence, in whatever circumstances, He has put into my heart and mind the inspiring words needed for the particular occasion.

One particular example may suffice: I was standing one morning in the shower, using the time for a period of thanks and praise addressed to my God. Suddenly and quite involuntarily I said aloud, 'If only I might see You as You are rather than in images.' Before I could reflect upon what I had dared to say, a clear voice broke through the sound of rushing water: 'Read the first chapter of Corinthians again, verses 4 to 7.' I was very familiar with those words. As I reread them, a flash of insight revealed my God and I knew that to see Him face to face would mean death. God I saw more clearly than anything I had ever been shown of Him before, a God who is Love, the absolute essence of patience and kindness, the complete antithesis of jealousy and conceit, neither proud, ill-mannered, selfish or irritable. Further (contrary to what some theologians teach), He does not keep a record of my wrongs. He is not happy with evil but happy with truth. He never gives up. His faith in me, His hope for me and His patience with me will never fail.

It has taken fifty years of my life to be able to say 'Whereas I was blind, now can I see Him whom I worship.'

I hope the foregoing will be of encouragement to the increasing number of men, women and children who are in this age learning that

> When man listens, God speaks,
> When man obeys, God acts;
> When God acts, miracles happen.

MULTIPLE EXPERIENCES

*

The people who have written of multiple experiences sometimes write as if they have come to welcome them like friends. They have come to live with more than one dimension in their lives, and regard this as not unusual.

Some people have similar experiences each time, i.e., usually triggered by nature or music. Others have very different experiences from one time to the next.

The experiences in this chapter are ordered only in this way: those with always similar experiences, and those with always differing ones. As with any other categorization, we make no interpretation or judgement, or give any order of priority. We let the accounts stand as they are and let them convey what the writers themselves had put into them.

M. 74 (15–21. 36–45)   904

When I was living in Greece, I had the following experience on a dozen occasions or more. Each time I was alone and confronted by a beautiful landscape or (less often) by a brilliant starlit night. The first symptom was a sudden hush that seemed to envelop me – this was subjective, however, as my hearing and all my other senses appeared actually to be keener than normal. Then, almost at once, I had a strange feeling of expansion, which I find very difficult to describe. It seemed to me that, in some way, I was extending into my surroundings and was becoming one with them. At the same time I felt a sense of lightness, exhilaration and power, as if I was beginning to understand the true meaning of the whole Universe.

Unfortunately, this state never lasted for very long (only a few minutes, I think), as it was easily dispelled by any sudden sound – in one case by a dog barking in the distance. But the sense of exhilaration would often persist for half an hour or more. I use the expression 'exhilaration' and not 'ecstasy' because I always remained completely aware of my surroundings and could have 'broken the spell', had I wanted to do so, just by moving.

I have tried to observe if any 'laws' could be discerned, and have made the following tentative list.

1 I was always alone.
2 I was always in the presence of great natural beauty.
3 The feeling came on suddenly and could never be induced.
4 Heat appeared to help, i.e., warm summer weather, usually around noon.
5 A pleasant monotonous sound helped. The singing of cicadas, the wind through pine branches, the lisp of a quiet sea.
6 A pleasant fragrance also helped, especially that of wild thyme. In one case (night and stars) a nearby lemon orchard.

I have described this latter experience in the following lines, which, perhaps, sum up the situation better than prose.

> Sky and reflecting sea with stars were filled,
> A lemon orchard in the nearby gloom
> Exhaled its fragrance, and a cricket trilled.
> And every essence by the night distilled
> – Scent, starlight, sound – was woven on a loom

Of transmutation, twining me till I
Had blended into earth and sea and sky . . .

F. 28 (21, 24) 2668

I am very pleased to have the opportunity to tell you of my 'religious' experience, although I do not know whether it is exactly religious.

It is a feeling of absolute oneness with nature, which sweeps over me unexpectedly and, unfortunately, only lasts for four or five minutes. I have only had this feeling twice in my life so far, once at 21 and once at 24, and it only seems to come on when I am on my own and out in the country admiring some scenery. I am a part of nature itself and it is a part of me – we are one. And all the scenery I am looking at is mine – a part of me. Nothing else matters, there are no worries or fears and everything is perfectly peaceful. Nothing matters but this. And when I die it will be the same. I could die right then and it wouldn't matter. I will never 'die' as such.

I have often tried to get this feeling back, but it cannot be made to come on.

My religious upbringing was not very strict. I went to Sunday school as a child but since then have hardly ever been to church, although I still believe in God, or at least a powerful force. I do not and cannot believe that death is the end.

M. 50 (20, 23, 42) 3401

I do not know whether or not the experiences which I shall attempt to relate can correctly be described as religious ones. They were certainly strange, compelling, powerful and utterly unforgettable.

The first one occurred when I was serving in a newly commissioned ship, which had been sent to the base for what were called 'working-up' exercises. I went ashore alone one evening and walked away from the town along the path which leads to the lighthouse. It was a most beautiful evening, with a pearly sea and sky and touches of pink on the clouds and in the water. I became aware of – rather than heard – indescribably beautiful music, almost too far away to grasp, yet at the same time pervading the whole of the land and sea and sky. All sense of time disappeared.

I do not think at that time I had ever heard any of the music of Delius, but five years later the whole episode was vividly re-created for me when I first heard 'A Song of the High Hills'.

When I got to know Elgar's 'The Dream of Gerontius', I felt I knew exactly what the Soul of Gerontius meant at the lines:

> And hark! I hear a singing: yet in sooth
> I cannot of that music rightly say
> Whether I hear, or touch, or taste the tones.
> Oh, what a heart-subduing melody!

Three years later I was on holiday with some friends. One afternoon I was walking, alone, downhill, and the prospect before me was a wide expanse of sky and sea shimmering under the afternoon sun.

Again, all sensation of time disappeared – or rather I felt that time had become frozen. There was also a feeling of the cessation of all sound. The shimmering of the water was extended to a quivering and throbbing of the whole physical universe, but this quivering seemed to be frozen in the sense of not taking part in time.

Since then I have had many walking and climbing holidays. I have stood on mountain tops and hoped for, longed for, experiences like the ones I have attempted to describe. But each time I have gone away with the feeling that I am now too much tainted by the ways of the world to enter into that state of revelation ever again.

The third experience was more recent and rather different from the others.

I was 42 at the time and giving tea to a pupil of mine – a boy of 15 – who was an exceptionally talented organist and has since become one of the leading young organists in the country.

While we had tea we listened to a broadcast organ recital. The organist was playing a Bach fugue. Opposite me, on a wall bracket, was an ivy plant spreading down two or three feet below the pot. As I looked at it, the ivy and the fugue became the same thing, or rather different expressions of the same thing: each explained the other.

M. 53 (?)   2461

The two experiences related have done far more to bring home to
me the oneness of the cosmos than anything else. As a result of
these, I am neither atheist, or theist, or agnostic in any of the
recognized meanings of those words. I am convinced, however, that
life transcends the physical in some way we comprehend only in
the dimmest way except in these momentary flashes which I feel
sure must be common to all minds sufficiently open to appreciate
the nature of the revelation.

I had been to an orchestral concert given by our local orchestra
and had enjoyed it very much. In those days good music stimulated
my emotions to the extent that I perspired excessively, but otherwise
there was no outward sign of any abnormal mental state that anyone
else would notice. The walk home was a distance of a half to three
quarters of a mile. About 200 or 300 yards from my home it
suddenly happened. It was a slightly frosty night and the sky was
very clear. On such nights I was in the habit of ranging the sky for
the few constellations I could recognize. On reaching the particular
spot something happened which I am sure I shall find great
difficulty in describing. If you can imagine yourself not as a
photographic flash bulb but as the light from that bulb and that the
light is sentient, that is the nearest I can get to explaining how I felt
at that moment. I was perfectly conscious of where I was and of my
immediate physical surroundings, but for that brief moment it was
as though my whole self was able to expand to and encompass the
furthermost star. It was an influx of a certain knowledge in that one
flash, that somewhere in the make-up of the cosmos is a factor
which transcends time and distance.

The second experience occurred one fine autumn morning when
I was digging potatoes. I was in a small field edged with hedges
and trees. This time the 'expansion' was, geographically speaking,
more limited, but none the less vivid. For an equally immeasurable
short length of time it was as though my real self was as much in
the surrounding natural scene as in my physical body and as though
everything was suffused with an unnatural brilliance and vitality.

In both cases you could liken it to a kind of bilocation, but, to
coin a contradictory term, it was more like total-location.

F. ? (?) 3062

I have had many beautiful experiences, but the most beautiful appears frequently. I can be driving in my car, walking down the street, working in my garden, etc., when all round me literally glows with light, colours become absolutely vibrant and such a tremendous feeling of Divine Love washes over me I feel attuned in perfect harmony with every living being in the universe.

My life has been greatly changed. Animals come to me, people have written me and stopped me on lecture platforms and asked where the radiating light around me comes from. The only answer I can give is God. God is love, and if we become filled with true love for all things around us, we must radiate that love in our auras.

F. 72 (32) 4113

I was matron in a boys' school. It was in a country village and when I was off duty in the afternoon there was nothing to do but go for a walk, go into church or have a quiet time in my room.

One day as I knelt by the fire, my elbows on a chair, I lost the sensation of having a body. I felt a presence across the room and to go nearer I had to pass through a white fire. My spirit did this without feeling anything except happiness and gratitude. The Presence said 'Remember this when you feel you don't belong to me' and I said (in my mind) 'How can I ever feel I don't belong to you' He(?) looked at me and again told me to remember and I thought 'I could never forget.' Then I felt Him leaving, and said, 'Won't you come again?' There was a slight pause and He said 'Not like this', and was gone.

I was back in my body, gazing across the room, and I felt so full of joy and peace I felt my face must be shining like Moses', but I looked no different.

Years later I had a bad time of anxiety and depression and felt that a high wall separated me from God. I was very unhappy – for a long time. Then I remembered what had happened years before and I think that helped the wall to disappear gradually.

On another occasion I was with a small group and we were finishing a devotional meeting with the Lord's Prayer. Suddenly my spirit was up in the sky and huge clouds were separating to make a wide clear road. There was a noise like thunder and I asked what it meant – and the thunder turned into a loud voice saying 'The Kingdom, the power and the glory', and I was back in my body to hear people say, 'for ever and ever, Amen'. I never told anybody about this.

F. ? (?)   2072

I don't remember this myself, but my mother told me of it – at least I don't *think* I do.

When I was quite small I was found on my own vigorously turning a skipping rope tied to the end of a bed. (I was an only child and mostly did play alone, a useful accomplishment!) Asked what I was at, I said 'I've got God in here. While he's here, I know where I have him.'

I cannot, in fact, remember a time when I doubted God as real and a person, when I was not aware of him. This has at certain times been an awareness that has shaken me in soul and body and with the utmost profundity – with love, yes, but even more with the mere fact of this superhumanly *real* person who confronts me, too real, sometimes, for me to bear to stay there – Barth's 'shattering halt in the presence of God'.

This happened one evening in the rather odd digs where I was evacuated with my school. We were walking through the village after a harvest supper (a new one on a Londoner) and the sunset was splendid and it was all rather fun, but I knew I must get away alone before I betrayed myself. I did, and the experience is now expressible in the terms below, though then they would have been different. It was only a bit later that I realized this had to issue in testing my vocation in the community of which I am still a member: that evening, the personal transaction was the whole thing.

Two years ago in an empty railway carriage I said again and again, for I don't know how long, 'You, you, you, my God, you . . .' Afterwards I put it like this:

You,
over against me,
more real than I,
existing from always.
You, the initiative,
the Sustainer of being.

You,
confronting and challenging,
compelling my attention,
yet often ignored,
with no diminishment
    of your being.

You.
In that simple address
is all the whole.

You.
Austere regard,
Severe, clean outline,
total consummation –
You.

Clay to potter!
Woodlouse to Ginstein!
Blackbeetle to ballerina!
This is love –
That such can stand up,
and say –
    You.

Since then one of my definitions of real prayer has been 'saying *you* to God'. (I had not then read 'I and Thou' – I have now, many times!)

The other facet of this is his presence in people. This I wrote about seven years ago.

Christmastide Post-Communion

I went quickly from the Lord's table
To catch an early train,
And moved with the work-bound crowds
With the thought of the Word made flesh
In the stable, on the altar.

> In the carriage, a workman in working clothes,
> His strong workman's hands at rest,
> His haversack and flask by his side.
>
> And I thought, 'Such, in his day, was Christ –
> But should I know him, if I had seen him thus?
> – Nay –
>   *do* I know him,
>   now that I see him thus?'

(badly quoted, I think – from memory)

Now, the proper attitude for prayer is *either* the most relaxed I can achieve (regardless of elegance) or the ancient one with head up and hands held out – either being a bodily expression of my awareness of the other whom I am meeting.

At such times he often is found beside me saying quite prosaically, 'Go ahead and don't worry. It's only me.' And 'It's only me' has become another key word.

F. 84 (some years ago; two years ago)   433²

I was just coming into my lounge and something stopped me, which seemed to come up from the floor at my feet and came up through my body and I saw the Lord in front of me. I stood there fixed for a minute or two; what a funny feeling it was. But after that I felt a different person, everything has changed now, I know I have an unseen friend and guide.

This happened some years ago. Then about two years ago I was going into the other room and Christ appeared above the door, but just a passing glance and it was gone. I shall never forget this 'spiritual experience', because it has helped me such a lot, wherever I go he gives me confidence, and I try to explain to my daughters about this, for without God I am nothing.

I wish many more would think a little; it does so help as life goes on. I am so glad I can tell this to somebody.

F. ? (?) 2657

To my brother and sister and myself God was a judge who sat upon a throne, his long white beard flowing and his piercing eyes watching each and every one of those who had been fortunate upon Earth to live a blameless life and who at the time of my childhood sang nightly and daily around a starry throne.

He could also see each of us, too, at the same time as watching the heavenly host. This alone filled me with awe. I was about 4 years old when a preacher shouted and raved, thumping the wooden pulpit, telling us that unless we renounced the Devil we would be cast into the bottomless pit, where flames which burned eternally would torment us forever.

However, as I grew older and was spared the punishment which I was convinced I deserved, I began to read my Bible and realized that God was not really as bad as the old preacher had made out, and I remember how when I was about 12 I would gabble through my prayers at night and then would add, 'And I know *you will realize* I didn't *really* mean to knock my sister out of the tree' or whatever miserable deed I had committed.

Very, very slowly, then, God became someone to whom I could talk. He was no longer the old man with the beard, but as I grew to realize that God and Jesus were really the same, my picture of God changed. It was to Christ I turned when I was worried or unhappy.

During the Second World War my husband was taken ill and I found him in hospital many miles from home. I had with me our four-year-old son. The sirens were sounding and I was truly afraid for my little son and, indeed, for my own safety. Worried sick over my husband, I said to my boy, 'If only Daddy could be with us.' He turned to me and said 'Let's tell gentle Jesus'. He knelt and said a simple little prayer, the all clear sounded and we telephoned the hospital to ask after my husband. He was very much better and could leave the hospital that very night if I could be with him.

It was too much to realize that God had indeed answered that simple little prayer.

My son grew up and at 18 sat for his A level examinations.

I well remember how I stood at my bedroom window and, thinking about the examination, I suddenly saw my boy seated at a desk and by his side with a hand on his shoulder stood a figure, which appeared to be clothed in the garb of an Arab. It was so real that I wanted to walk over towards them. I saw the long flowing robe, the white cowl over the head and bare feet with leather sandals. Then, slowly the figure turned and the face was so beautiful – I have never seen a picture which contained such an expression of love and sympathy. Yet I felt no fear, only a deep glow of warmth and peace.

The boy passed his exams and gained entrance to university. It was at the time of conscription and the university could not take him for another year. My son joined the regiment of the Guards and within five months of leaving grammar school he was posted abroad, where every day we heard news of loss of life. There was no sense in becoming too unhappy but I was very worried.

Then one evening as the setting sun glowed on a picture of my son, I saw once again the hooded figure with a hand on the boy's shoulder. I knew that all would be well with him. He came safely home and, with his two friends who had been at school with him, studied for more exams. The two friends would come to me and say 'I have a big exam on such a date – please pray for me.' One is now a barrister, another a very good doctor.

Almost every time I prayed for them, I would see the figure, which I had come to know as Christ.

Two years ago my husband was seriously ill. There was little hope; he had a brain haemorrhage. I walked alone from the hospital where I had to leave him. I was miles from home and from my children; I did not even know where I was going to spend the night. Into my mind came those words 'My God, why hast Thou forsaken me?' With my head bowed and the tears blurring my sight, I saw a brown sandal and, as I walked, the figure beside me began to take shape. I felt a strong hand on my shoulder and then it had gone. But my heart was comforted and I went straight to the nearest church and asked for God to keep my husband in His care.

My husband proved to be almost a miracle case. He is now walking and talking and enjoying life as much as possible while I live each day in the hope of when the journey of life is over and the shadows fall, I shall place my hand in the hand of Him who has given me courage and who will lead me to the GREAT ADVENTURE.

F. 26 (?)

For as long as I can remember I have had the feeling that there is an unseen hand guiding me. My husband and friends often hear me say jokingly 'My guardian angel is watching me.' I do not have an explanation of this feeling but I have a constant experience of calm.

Two years ago my grandmother died. After her death I had a sense of her being with me. Shortly after her death I was driving my car to work and I unfortunately crashed into a tree. The traffic was not particularly heavy, but it was misty and I must have entered a sudden blanket of fog.

The car was not too seriously damaged, but I received serious internal injuries. I was taken to hospital, where, I have since been informed, the doctors did not think I would live through that day. However, I had an operation and survived. I remember no pain. I remember feeling comforted all the time.

Towards the middle of my stay in hospital I was aware of a face looming over me. This showed such a gentle smile. Suddenly my grandmother came to me, she kissed my eyes and told me I would be all right. She took my hand and started to take me up. We reached a fence, which we did not cross. I could see clearly the other side and could tell anybody what it was like.

Another form came to me, an uncle of my husband's, who died the year before. This time he took my hand and told me it wasn't time yet. We went down and I woke up. I struggled to keep awake, but lapsed again into sleep and my grandmother appeared again and the procedure was repeated. On awakening the second time I managed to keep awake, frightened and convinced that the experience I had just faced was not a dream and was not the influence of drugs.

None of my family are church-goers. We were all christened Church of England. I have felt drawn to the Church from an early age and I still attend.

I feel a deep compassion towards sick people.

I realize, logically, that my outlook could be the result of my Christian feelings. My experience in hospital could have been the result of my binding to the Church, it could have been drugs, it could have been a dream.

The experience is lodged so vividly in my mind that I prefer to believe that I did experience this happening. It has strengthened my belief in God and life after death.

My husband is not a religious person; I do not discuss my feelings on this with him. I work and have a responsible job. I say this to help show that I am in no way a religious fanatic.

F. 65 (?)   2643

From the age of 18 I have had numerous 'experiences'; none of them has been religious.

A quite separate 'experience', if one can call it such, is that for many years I have had someone with me to whom I can refer if I need help, or the answer to a question or a problem. If I have put something away in the house and can't remember where, I have only to ask and I get an immediate picture in my mind of the whereabouts of the object. I look in this place and there is the thing I have been looking for. The 'presence' I lean on is a man and I call him by name.

I am basically a practical person, a professional secretary and in print this looks 'way out'. It is, nevertheless, fact.

I have seen ghosts, felt presences and seen the spirits (if that is what they are called) of live people actually in another room at the time. And I'm not a nut case!

I lived in an old vicarage which had a positive 'presence' felt by me, the rest of the family and friends who visited us. He was so positive everyone called him 'Fred'!

F. 80 (?)   2568

I am a great believer in prayer. I have often had doubts, but something soon happens to eliminate that. I have had so many answers that I couldn't recount them all, but I never ask for anything frivolous. In any difficulty I ask and I receive. Last year I could hardly walk. Now I walk normally. I've lost important things in the home and failed to find them. I ask and they turn up. I have a bedsitter and had trouble with insects in my bed, such as an earwig or small beetle. I asked and since have seen none. I had a little trouble with an electric gadget one day. I asked for help and a knock came at the door. A friend had unexpectedly called and soon put matters to right. You will know what this means when I tell you that I am over 80 years old and live alone. I ask for sleep when going to bed and I get eight hours almost every night. I am rather nervous, so I ask for help and a deep peace comes upon me. I prayed hard for a friend who was very ill. She recovered and the doctor said it was a miracle. These are only a few of the things that have happened to me, as I have been helped all my life. If I get no reply, I accept it as a part of God's wisdom. We do not give our own children everything they ask for. I have been helped in big things, too, but small things are important, as they prove your trust in God.

F. ? (?) 143

My experiences, few and far between, have taken the form of voices speaking to me, always when I am in a state of desperate anxiety. This is understandable, as in the ordinary business of living the ethic of one's own creed is adequate and sometimes one's contemporary friends come to the rescue. But there are times when both these sources of comfort break down and it is on such occasions that I have received direct help 'from above'.

The latest was a few years ago when I was quite desperate. I was alone in my house and a voice said to me 'You're all right, you old kettledrum.' This is an expression I should never use myself. Long ago, on a different occasion, a voice said quite clearly 'Don't be frightened', and again another time 'You are wanted where you are', and again 'Let yourself go, let me hold you', and again 'I am going to back you up'.

I am a very ordinary person except that I have had perhaps more than the ordinary amount of responsibility, having been headmistress of a girls' high school and subsequently have held high positions in local government, and in the course of domestic duties have been with four of my friends during their final illness and death.

F. 80 (?)

I do not remember a time when I was not aware of a presence which those around me did not sense. I had a sort of communion with a guiding voice within. It came to my aid in my childish problems, suggesting what I should do, certainly telling me within what was right and what was wrong, helping me to bear injustices without striving against them or retaliating against the wrongdoers.

During the growing-up period all the usual perplexities of the soul assailed me. I loved one young man, he most proper *but* not a Christian. That inner voice said, 'Be ye not unequally yoked together with unbelievers.' In my sorrow I told God about it and asked Him to give me the right husband. After one year He did so. We had three sons and strove to serve God, wishing that daily we might adorn His holy gospel.

Now I am living alone, my Heavenly Father meets all my small needs. The voice within is still my counsellor – it is the Holy Spirit. Some of the things which happened were termed 'miracles', but Christ says 'According to your faith be it unto you!'

> When we walk with the Lord,
> In the light of His word,
> What a glory He sheds on the way.
> When we do His sweet will
> He abides with us still
> And with all who will trust and obey.

F. ? (thirteen years ago, five years ago)   4404

I have felt what I thought was the peace of God. It occurs usually when I am most distressed. The first time was thirteen years ago when my daughter was born. She was my first child and, naturally, I was a bit bewildered by it all. However, she was jaundiced and after a couple of days she was taken away. I didn't realize then it was quite common, and no one bothered to explain to me what was happening and I got myself into a right state. That's when I noticed the Gideon Bible in a bracket on the wall. So I took it out and read the 'Where to find' index at the beginning. To this day I don't know what I read. I've never been able to find it again. But as I read the particular passage, a great feeling of peace came over me and I knew everything was going to be all right. Words can't adequately explain it. I was frightened half out of my mind, crying all over the place and then suddenly this calm, peaceful feeling took over, something told me my daughter was going to be all right.

Another time that stands out in my mind was maybe about five years ago. My husband and I had split up and my life was in a right mess. I was in the back garden hanging out the washing. I felt lost, confused; I didn't understand what was happening, where I was going, how I would manage. I felt I just couldn't go on and I just sat down, right there in the middle of the garden. Again for a moment that calm, peaceful feeling took over and something told me everything would be all right.

The feeling doesn't stay with you, it's only there for a second or so, but you're given the strength and knowledge to carry on. Maybe that's what it means in the Bible where it tells you you won't be given a burden too heavy to carry.

For me it's the Peace of God, and I thank him each time I feel it.

M. 80 (?)   2009

My experience, here and since my wife went, was right out of my life, but I believe now that it is something that I, personally, have missed years ago and in consequence it has been used to help others around this place; but that is not easy either.

My family were all believers, but I have deviated somewhat years ago until, possibly, during the 1914 war, when in a big action in the North Sea when hell seemed to be let loose. Suppose I was scared stiff, because I prayed briefly to God. But got out of that lot and, later, married a true believer. The first Sunday evening we went to church. Was dark and found ourselves in a very nice church building. The true gospel was preached, when suddenly the Pastor exclaimed '... would like all to dedicate themselves to God now and those who would do so to stay behind'. We stayed after a few whispers. We gave ourselves to God with sincerity – did not truthfully understand, but we kept our word.

We were young and working then, but we went to see Canon C.

That reverend gentleman quizzed us and we went to see a 'missioner' at a Jewish Hall. Well, we joined the mission band (eight of us). My first job was to visit and talk to the men in the 'doss' houses; did not think much of that at first, had never seen anything like it (but that is a story of its own). All this during weekends, of course, and just little after our marriage. However, we gradually got the confidence of those men. But the point is that I knew we could not possibly do this work without God's help, so suppose we thought we knew God and His ways – well, we did not as I now know.

My wife was taken 31 December suddenly; no illness, no suffering; we just parted after nearly fifty years of love, palship and one in Christ. Of course, one's grief becomes intense – but it is just one's own, no sharing; yet I had to come to grips with things, so I prayed and prayed to God because I did not want to leave our home. Am not ashamed of my prayer; it was that as I was now totally dependent upon Him I should need His help in practically everything. The message I received is written down in my Bible. Gradually I was aware of an intense love for God and a burning faith in His word, so I kept mine. I live as He wants us to live; may have skidded now and then but it hasn't been easy, as I really am rather gregarious. After all, Christ told us such would be the case.

Have now lived alone every night, without a visitor, for over four years and have always been happy and joyful in Christ. Neighbours have remarked on this – in fact, one said quite frankly 'Wish I had your faith'. And with some of these little 'curiosities' of people there seems to be a pathetic hunger and yearning after *true* (so very true) friendship and religion. When I get into real difficulties, and I do, it's prayer to God that solves these things. When I mislay things, and that is done so often, I ask God to find things for me and he does; I try first, mind. Have had two severe colds, with bad temperature; have prayed to God and He just cures them without any human aid. My neighbours will vouch for these things. After all, one does just simply take Jesus Christ at His word. In my experience of just trying to live as God wants us to live, in truth and honesty, there really is no need of loneliness amongst elderly folk and certainly not with the young.

After marriage, my work, for which I trained hard, was physio-therapy; was in practice twenty years. After much thought, went entirely on my own and built up a practice and when one gives treatment (not pills, drugs, etc. but infrared rays, ionization, manipulation and massage – which latter seems to be real 'laying on of hands'), to about twenty-five people each week, one gets to know people – and love them; and that is a very main reason why one really knows the love of Christ. A reverend man of God could give a fine sermon on that experience. In that work alone, irrespective of the religious side, one has seen the hand of God and one has also experienced the love, yes, clean love, of very many people. Makes one humble, you know.

Was paid for my work, but one thanks God that one has been able to do that work.

F. ? (nine and eight years ago) 4327

My husband had arthritis in his right arm. It was so painful he was finding driving difficult and could no longer lift with the right hand. Doctor's pills (twice) had not helped.

One evening he and I and a friend were talking over coffee after a very blessed day of services in our church. It was Whit Sunday. D was rubbing his arm. The friend suddenly said that he didn't feel Jesus wanted D to have that pain and should we pray about it. We hesitated; it was a new idea to us. We considered in silence. D said 'Yes, I'm ready', so we all repented before God and then J and I put our hands on D and I said something like 'Lord Jesus, we know you can heal D's arm. Please do it now.' And He did, at that very moment. That was eight years ago. The pain hasn't returned.

Twice God has 'spoken' to me when I have been in a large group silently praying in repentance for our sins. Both times it has been something I wouldn't have done and which seemed out of place almost. The first time I felt He was telling me to give up smoking and I said no. But the next day I stopped smoking and haven't had a cigarette since. Each time it was hard I prayed an arrow prayer such as 'Lord, it was your idea, please help.'

The second time, as the leader drew the repentance to an end and my heart had felt very stony and unable to think of my sins, I suddenly found myself to be sobbing and saying, 'Never mind me,

Lord, I'll go to hell if only you'll save them', 'them' being three of my six sons and daughters, who are not yet committed Christians.

As I look forward to Heaven I can only believe that God put that cry into my heart and that He will answer my prayers for them.

Another evening I was kneeling saying my prayers and I fell asleep. When I awoke the Lord Jesus was standing beside me. I could see the hem of His garment, but I didn't look up. I knew He was waiting for me to wake up and return to my prayer to Him, and I also knew that He was always waiting for me, whatever I was doing, to return to Him in thought and prayer. And what was most impressive, I could feel love emanating from Him – something I could not have imagined, it was a quite new experience. I felt ashamed and unworthy and wanted to crawl under the bed. It was a long time before I told anyone, but I treasured it and still do in my heart.

M. 37 (?)   874

For many years I have been aware of a need for some form of spiritual fulfilment. In common with many others with whom I have discussed this problem I find myself totally unable to accept the Church's teaching in the form in which it is currently presented. The clergymen I have talked to have been most sympathetic and equally unhelpful. It seems to me that they are afraid or unwilling to come out from behind the skirts of their dogma and, until they do so, I fear that they will be unable to make the most of man's latent spirituality.

I consider myself fortunate that experiences of a spiritual or religious nature have occurred quite frequently during my life. However, it is only within the last two years that I have begun to realize the significance of these experiences. Broadly speaking, there are two categories of experience involved. The first, and most common one, seems to be that in which music plays an important part. When listening to some of the works of Bach, Beethoven, Chopin and others, I feel an overwhelming sense of awe that these wonderful sounds could have been conceived within the mind of a mortal being. I would go further and say that during the presentation of the music I often find myself thinking that the composers themselves did not actually 'invent' the music but acted merely as the instrument to transcribe on to paper the sounds that they were fortunate enough to be able to hear in their inner mind. The net result is a sense of awe and of wonder and of joy that I belong to the same race as these giants of music and can appreciate the results of their inspiration howsoever caused.

The same feeling, to a lesser degree, is engendered when I read some forms of poetry. I feel that the musician and the poet are, in a particular way, allowing us a glimpse of their souls.

The second form of experience that I have is far more personal and infinitely more inspiring than the first. Although it is not a common experience, I find that I can induce it, after a certain amount of effort, the effect being so long lasting that once or twice in a year is sufficient to carry me through all the sort of day-to-day problems which beset us.

The phenomenon invariably occurs out of doors, more often than not when I am alone, although it has occurred when I have been in company with others. It is generally prefaced by a general feeling of 'gladness to be alive'. I am never aware of how long this feeling persists but after a period, I am conscious of an awakening of my senses. Everything becomes suddenly more clearly defined; sights, sounds and smells take on a whole new meaning. I become aware of the goodness of everything. Then, as though a light were switched off, everything becomes still and I actually feel as though I were part of the scene around me. I can identify with the trees or the rocks or the earth and, with this identification and the tremendous stirring within me, it seems as though I am looking at the human race, and myself in particular, through the wrong end of a telescope. I feel as though I have the power to do anything, no problem is too great for me to tackle – and with this feeling comes an ineffable sense of peace and well-being.

Just as suddenly as it began, it ceases and I find myself back, as it were, in reality again, with the exception that the feeling of peace and well-being remains with me and stays with me sometimes for many weeks. Unlike the experience which occurs in the presence of great music, and which often makes me feel close to tears, this latter experience seems to have no emotional involvement whatever other than a desire to be more tolerant, which is perhaps another way of showing more love to others.

Until two years ago I accepted this latter experience for what it was and was just jolly thankful that it happened. Since then, however, I have tried to analyse it, with some amazing results. I found that by considering certain objectives I can induce the experience at will, although not always to the extent of identifying with my surroundings. The feeling of well-being occurs, however, whether the experience is self-induced or whether it occurs spontaneously.

Although I am not a conventionally religious person, I came to the conclusion that the 'stillness and identifying' stage of the experience would be what a mystic or member of the clergy might call 'the presence of God'. Further, because I cannot bring myself to accept a God who is totally outside us as persons, I concluded that it was God within me who was making His presence felt. This latter point has proved of tremendous comfort to me because, by means of my experience, I have a direct line of communication to God, which no amount of praying or church-going would bring me.

I have used the word 'God' because I know of no other word which carries the implication of infinite power, goodness, wisdom and peace. But whatever name we give to this power, there is absolutely no doubt in my mind that it exists and that it is available to anyone who is prepared to expend some effort to make contact. I am convinced, too, as a result of my experiences, that conscious thought survives death of the physical body.

I would like nothing better than the opportunity to try to pass on to others my method of inducing an 'experience'. However, experiments with my family have not been at all successful. It seems to me that experiences of this kind are intensely personal. My early upbringing was by my grandparents, who were strict Presbyterians. Subsequently I became confirmed into the Church of England, but my actual church-going lapsed when I realized that it was doing nothing for me other than making me feel that I was a hypocrite.

F. ? (?)   1143

In February of this present year, after a long period of trial and distress, I had gone early to bed, in New Zealand.

It was a warm and quiet summer evening. Still light and unable to sleep, I lay on my back, when suddenly my eyes, as it were, compelled by some sudden intuition, were wrenched open and my gaze borne upwards. I observed hovering above me a shape tremendously luminous, bearing around the edges a flare of gold. Filled with awe (I was transfixed), I watched this hovering shape (shapeless, like a field of energy) from which issued a *roar* or *vibrant sound* and a most awesome force beyond description.

I felt myself drawn up and at the same time borne down upon, as if I would become it and by it be possessed and at the *same time I intuitively sensed this shape in some way to be myself.*

So mighty and beautiful was this 'visitant' and so awesome the power it generated that, feeling I might die, I cried out and it vanished. These manifestations of our mysterious destiny take courage to witness, being of a nature as yet unknown to us. But from my heart, in the days that followed, rose a great and joyous 'hosanna', for I felt I had seen some light in the wilderness and there is hope that man may find the wisdom yet to develop this other and furthest shore of his destiny. As far as it being as fundamental as sex, I would suggest we misunderstand this term and its related energy, which in our narrow society we give a limiting biological meaning.

Previous to this advent I saw in the full glare of the afternoon light, while watching TV in a very desultory way, a little irritated and bored, the slim shape of a man pass, as I thought, across the terrace windows very swiftly and traverse past the other three, and in annoyance at this intrusion I got up to open the last remaining window and reprimand the intruder, when it vanished completely and instantly, and I realized that this shape had remained all the time pressed *flat* against the windows and glass and was entirely black like a rubbed-out charcoal drawing.

Perhaps I should have been more methodical about writing this and told you that my first experience in these things occurred about twenty years ago, in a room where a rather tense and charged family debate was taking place and I was feeling my powers of love and compassion very strained.

That room was suddenly illumined by an all-enveloping light of strange intensity and I felt myself 'opened' and all consciousness of the ground beneath my feet disappear while a tremendous ecstasy, greater than the ecstasy of love, flooded my whole being. The people present in the room became very distant, as though a long way off, and it seemed that everything, even in that destructive moment of dissent, made a most serene and final 'sense'.

M. ? (?)   4548

I begin by making clear that I am not sensitive to the point of being what is called 'psychic' – I do not experience premonitions or any such thing. But I have always had a deep spiritual awareness, hence, I suppose, my eventual vocation to the priesthood, in which I have served for some forty years. All pretty hard work – marvellous.

However, more to the point would be my meditation in my early days as a curate in wartime south London. Of a sudden, I was suffused with what I can only describe as an internal explosion of light. It lasted the merest fraction of a second or so, but in that time one was given what I can only describe as a Dame Julian of Norwich view of all existence and its ultimate transfiguration with the knowledge that 'all manner of thing would be well'. It was an experience during which one's comprehension seemed to achieve a kind of cosmic dimension.

My subsequent reaction – having been at a rather low ebb – was to be hesitantly restored. Life around me was somehow lighter in both meanings of the word. Particularly, I found this world to be very gross – large, clumsy – almost unbelievably so. My remembrance of it remains green.

At another time I was holidaying in Switzerland and, taking a walk, was pondering, of all things, the Kantian theory of knowledge. I was much younger then and an enthusiastic philosopher as a means to get closer to reality. Somehow my arguments ended in a theory of energy as being behind all phenomena – nothing special in that, of course, but having my mind latched on to the idea, again, quite suddenly the whole of that beautiful setting became music. It was indescribably beautiful – a vast sound, majestic yet not overpowering like the LPO at full chat.

Finally, many years later – about ten years ago now – I was working in G, a very tough assignment and demanding one's experience to the full. I had returned home for luncheon and my wife, normally punctual to the minute, was behind schedule, so I took the opportunity of putting on a Mozart quartet on my new hi-fi set, of which I was very proud.

I stood listening and at the same time looking out upon the street seven storeys below when, once more, of a sudden there entered into my listening awareness music of another kind, of another dimension: this time gentle but long enough for me objectively to consider the merits of the two kinds of music. I have to say that the sounds we produce here, felicitous though they may be, are of an incomparably coarser quality. If this existence should be a Platonic shadow world, I can only say that my experiences would have to declare the difference to be as great as between the giant flying reptiles of an age long past and the kingfisher or butterfly. The Te Deum consequently, perhaps, has been a staple of my devotional diet.

It ought to be mentioned, perhaps, that these experiences were of a transcendent nature, i.e., they were of a dimension not only beyond the present one but also, if one might put it so, they were, in their own way, of a superior kind.

Being an experience it was, of course, subjectively perceived, but it had been objectively imposed, which is also to include the fact that it was an experience which, as far as I was concerned, could not be subjectively induced nor could its duration be extended or manipulated by one's self. Thus, its objectivity seemed to be beyond debate.

There are many theories about such things and much to be explored, but one is given to wonder if they are evidences of what might await us beyond the fringes of our present state of evolution. We know the theories surrounding the idea of evolution differ, but taking a broad view and bearing in mind the vast time span involved, the signs seem to be that purposive change has been at work and man, by the very nature of things, cannot escape its consequences. Are we now in something of a chrysalis stage, one wonders? Are these experiences – occurring, as they do, to all kinds

– the signs of a new dawn for humanity? Well, one can ponder and speculate, but whatever it is, when these events happen, we are ushered into a beyondness which defies calculation.

F. 50 (22, 24, 45)   3670

Apart from various feelings of devoutness at the time of puberty, there have been three markedly outstanding religious experiences in my life.

I was aged about 22 and was sitting by myself in a room seldom used by the rest of the family, as I wanted to play my gramophone. While I listened to the music I was doing a little peaceful sewing. At one point I had on the Brahms' First Symphony (of which I am not especially fond) and was in a state of complete relaxation. However, a chord sounded and at once I was removed from my normal life. My whole physical being was dissolved and I knew that I was, in reality, a spiritual creature who only had the semblance of a body. I was, quite obviously, the note of music. Not only that, but I was also the light that shone a clear blue just to the left of my mental vision. Being thus totally non-physical scared me and at once I was reunited with my ordinary self and for some years preferred to forget the incident. (I did search for that chord, though, but never again found it.)

When I was aged 24 I was deeply involved in an emotional situation which, although bringing me a great deal of happiness, was causing me very deep distress, as the man I was in love with was treating me with what I now realize was almost complete selfishness, coupled with the inevitable mental cruelty. However, as I knew that he himself was undergoing a period of great stress and unhappiness, I tried to be understanding and forgiving at all times in the belief that if I was gentle, his bad time would pass. The time came, though, when I felt that I could really take no more, as I knew that I was being wronged and my meek acceptance of his injustices was not helping the situation. One day, during my lunch hour at work, I was sitting at my office desk with the intention of writing to him to protest at his treatment and to give vent to at least some of my pent-up resentment. As I sat, paper before me and pen in my hand, planning how to begin and which of my furies to unleash first, I rehearsed the words of my greatest grievance. As I mentally went through the details, a voice said to me quite clearly, 'And what are you going to do about it?'

I knew then (as I know now) that it was not the voice of mere 'conscience' – whatever that may be – but God. For one thing, the words were so ambiguous. If they had been my words, I would have answered that I was going to write a thundering great bomb of a letter because I wanted no more of the situation as it was. 'Write a letter' would have been the instant reply. But, instead, I knew that what I had to do was to go on – for ever, if necessary – being tolerant and patient and forgiving. My sense of injustice was not removed (I felt just as badly wronged as before) but gone was the wish to retaliate. So I put down my pen and I never did write that letter.

Another incident occurred, which has impressed me greatly, when I was 45. A friend of mine was very ill indeed and thought to be dying. Because of this, while on my usual weekly shopping trip, I went into the little side chapel in the cathedral. I don't believe in mere petitionary or intercessionary prayer (because how can I possibly tell what is best for myself or others?), so I was more intent in making available to God my own health and strength so that some of my energy force could be transferred to my friend whose own life-forces were weakening. (With the lesson of 'What are you going to do about it?' not yet forgotten, I was trying to do something practical instead of just sitting around expecting God to do everything all by Himself.)

As I sat quietly in the little chapel, I became aware that the massive solidity of those huge stone pillars was an illusion. Like my own body and that of my friend they were no more than pulsating columns of totally insubstantial atoms of power. It seemed that they were vibrating with a ceaseless manifestation of power – rather as a chord of music will vibrate in the air long after the player has ceased. Their solidity was total illusion. The whole universe was an illusion. There is nothing but pure Energy – nothing but God.

M. 28 (22, 26)   3191

Six years ago I was asleep in the night and began to feel the most
intense sensation of *Love*. It was a love for all other human beings,
and also a love given *to* me *by* other human beings. It was so
powerful that I can recall clearly the beauty and 'nobility' of the
sensation, and I still believe it to be one of the most significant
experiences to have affected my outlook on life. Yet it was
completely different to anything else I have ever felt.

I am not sure if I was completely awake, but certainly was awake
after the experience; it was probably very brief.

It seemed to be a *personalized* feeling, in the sense that I could
easily attribute such an influential sensation to another 'person',
e.g., God or Jesus (in whom I happen to believe).

The second experience was of equal power and lasting effect,
but more concrete. A year and a half ago I was asleep in the night
and woke very suddenly and felt quite alert. I felt surrounded and
threatened by the most terrifying and powerful presence of Evil. It
seemed to be localized within the room. It seemed almost physical
and in a curious way it 'crackled', though not audibly. It was also
extremely 'black', and I felt almost overwhelmed with terror. I
stayed rigid in my bed for several minutes wondering how to
combat this blackness. I felt it was a manifestation directed very
personally at me, by a Power of Darkness. I was overwhelmed by
despair and a desire to go out and kill myself by jumping in the
river nearby, but I knew I must withstand this.

I got a crucifix which was on the wall (I was staying at a monastic
guest-house) and commanded it to go away. So physical did it feel
that I wanted to close the open window to prevent it from re-
entering, if it had gone. I was shaking with fear and eventually
telephoned a friend to ask if I could go over. I dressed and ran
from the building.

When I went back to the room the following day I was still very
apprehensive!

I hasten to say that although I am a sensitive and sometimes
emotional person, I am usually sceptical about abstract phenomena!
I have not told many people of these experiences because of their
'melodramatic' sides. I have been as objective as I can in describing
them.

F. 41 (27, 37) 4711

There are many moments in my life when I am aware of a presence, moments perhaps of a closeness to God. But there are two such experiences which stand out. I have not talked about them much at all, because of their personal and intense nature, but I don't regard them as personal property either.

I had been in a convent nearly two years when I had finally decided to leave again. This was a Franciscan community. I had just talked to the Mother Superior and told her that I wanted to leave, and she agreed that I should. Relieved, I went into the chapel for a quick 'thank you' prayer. I was alone in the chapel, and then it was as if the Christ on the crucifix spoke to me. I could clearly hear him say, 'Your sins are forgiven.' I have always considered this a very 'Franciscan' experience, but for years I puzzled over the phrase. Had I sinned by leaving the convent or going in in the first place? Gradually, I have come to take the words themselves less literally and see them as an expression of Christ's complete acceptance and love.

The second very strong experience was a few years back. I was at the time very struck with the horror of the suicides in Jonestown in South America, where about 2,000 young people drank some poison. When this had happened, I had not seen any pictures, but about two years later I had read about it again in some report. It was some weeks after that that while at prayer I suddenly felt as if I had become one of them. I felt my whole body becoming rigid, the flesh go black and cold. I don't know how long this lasted (some minutes perhaps), but I was terrified and deeply disturbed. I felt in the grip of some evil force, which had got hold of me and which was quite unknown to me. At the time all my clergy friends were away or on holiday, so I wrote to a priest who I considered to be an expert in the field. He responded very quickly, reassuring me. In particular, he explained that in any such strong experience I would still be in charge. This has often helped me. As that experience was so strong and so frightening, I obviously remember it fairly often. When I do, I always pray for the people involved in that incident, but each time I come up against some force of darkness and resistance, which I don't encounter in the same way when praying for other sad situations. The fact that this had happened to me while I was praying makes me now feel that I have a certain responsibility, or 'call', to go on praying for these people.

F. 50 (?) 2074

Usual religious upbringing at school and church, but had never had any conscious effect on me. Had never heard of religious experiences or conversion experiences. Would have thought, if told of any of them, that people were 'round the bend' a little.

At this time after a divorce, had remarried and had a baby boy of 10 months, who had been ill with whooping cough. It was a Saturday morning and I was feeling very cold and tired and anything but religious when the vicar's wife called in to see how the baby was. She had a 'thing' on at that time about spiritual healing and wanted to say a prayer for the baby. I was rather embarrassed but we sat in my small dining-room and she said a prayer and I said 'Amen' and then was glad to get rid of her.

After she was gone, I thought, 'Why should God do anything for my baby; I have never done anything for him?' and stood in the dining-room. At that moment I felt that someone had entered the hall; the feeling grew until I felt the presence of a person, a *masculine real person*. I had the impression of someone slightly taller and broader than average and of tremendous strength of person-ality. A strength that was immutable, flowing out, from him. The previous moment I had been thinking of God and it seemed that this thought and the person were one. There was this Authority that was greater than me and greater than he, but he was equal with it, and one with it, although it was greater than him because it was wider and different, like a policeman who in uniform is the law, but the law is both wider and *one with him*, but above him. I felt all my life till this moment I had ignored this Authority but it had known *me* all the time, and here it was with everything added up. The feeling of the person grew until I felt him enter the room and place his hands on my shoulders. I sensed an *overwhelming* compassion in him, and something terribly sad over something that was about to happen to me. It was as if it were not of his fault, but of my own momentum, moving to an inevitable conclusion which he was powerless to stop.

I felt the pressure of his hands and the same pressure very gently but firmly over my body, as if firming it together with strength. At the same time a current of warm vibrations flowed out of me. It seemed to flow in from him, yet at the same time rise up in *me*, flowing down my arms and out of my hands into a warm stream. Apart from this person connecting with the Authority that was all around, I did not think of him as anything supernatural or for one moment as Christ. He was a person who could have sat on a committee, nursed the baby or ran a business. He seemed connected to everything in life and understood it. I had to see if he was in other parts of the house, so I went in every room of our four-storeyed house. He was beside me all the time, yet seemed to be in the rooms before I entered and still there when I left. The whole house was filled with his presence. Soon my husband came in and everything went on as before, but the person was still there, even when I had been out shopping. A week later the baby was taken worse and died ten days later in hospital. After that the presence faded, but I seemed to be living on a new dimension, a little way above the Earth but still doing everything just the same. The *amazement* stayed with me for many years, that I was connected with this Authority and that it was concerned with *me*. I did not for years think that I had had an experience of Christ but after reading of other experiences, realized that that was what it could have been.

The second experience came about five years later. Life had gone on in various ways quite normally and at that particular time a tricky situation had arisen, which was troubling me greatly and had the effect of making me feel sick and faint. I had to go to London and dreaded it. I had taken a nip of brandy in my handbag in case I felt faint, and was sitting in the bus wondering how I would get through the day when I felt suddenly the presence of the same person standing by my seat. This time he was not sad and compassionate but full of joy at what was happening. As before, there was this connecting point between reality and him and the Authority that I felt to be God – and me. Instantly I relaxed and had the same strength flowing into me. I went through the day as if in a protective shell, feeling completely strong and calm. I have yet to discover why the situation was so pleasing to him; it wasn't to me!

About two years later I was in London with my husband for a

week's sightseeing. I had been in the cathedral about a minute when I felt a tremendous vibration coming from the walls of the cathedral. It was a terrific physical power pouring out from them and into me; at the same time it seemed to be coming from outside the cathedral from some source far away and greater than the space occupied by the cathedral. My body seemed to connect up with it and I was part of it and the cathedral was nothing. I sat through the service; all the time this current was connecting up and flowing through me until I felt as light bodily as a breath of air. This feeling lasted for many weeks, and many years after, I could get a similar vibration but much smaller whenever I entered any consecrated building, even a cemetery. I find that certain places have it much more than others.

For the last five years or so it seemed that all these experiences have faded and mean little to me. I try to remember them and make them mean what they seemed to mean at the time. Perhaps I have another experience to go through to see what good they have done me or what help I have been to God through them. At the moment I am spiritually at a low ebb, which seems a pity after all that!

F. ? (22–23)   2476

At the age of 22–23 I remember standing in my room when suddenly I felt 'dizzy' – overwhelmed by a sensation of 'light' – it felt as if flame was around me. It seemed as if I was transported on to another plane of consciousness, shot through with an almost unbearable Joy.

I don't know how long this experience lasted, maybe a few minutes or even only a few seconds: it did not belong to a time-space world. The sensation of joy and inexplicable happiness lasted two or three days, gradually fading. It happened at a time in my life when I was enjoying things enormously in a normal way.

Another time this same sort of experience happened was in France. One weekend I spent at a convent. There was Exposition of the Blessed Sacrament and as I knelt in obeisance in the aisle, this sensation happened again – a feeling of being surrounded by light and inexpressible happiness.

One might have thought that in a chapel this was definitely a religious experience, but the same sensation happened a few months later. I had gone out to get something for lunch and as I was passing a greengrocer I saw him weighing out Brussels sprouts – and it happened again! When I 'came to' he was still weighing sprouts, so the experience can only have lasted a few seconds, although I had gone clean out – it might have been a hundred years. These experiences have no relation to time. Again the sensation of happiness lingered with me for several days. Each time I wanted to be very quiet for some hours afterwards, as if I was adjusting myself from a shock.

I have never had any experiences of this particular kind since.

A different type of extra-sensory experience happened after my husband died. I had returned from the hospital and was resting on my bed at home in the afternoon when he was quietly there – not exactly physically but quite definitely at my side. He wanted to tell me not to worry or grieve too much, that he was happy, that 'all was well'. This happened five times within a few months after his death – in his study, in the garden, by my bedside and last time when I had gone to stay with friends. We were about to have lunch. The table was laid for three and suddenly he was there sitting opposite me, again not exactly physically, just an unmistakable presence.

Each time the experience was accompanied by physical sensations. I felt extremely cold, icy; the normal world seemed very remote, the connecting link had almost gone.

Another quite different super-sensory experience happened more recently. I went to a school of meditation. The conferences were conducted by P, trained in India and the Sikh School of Meditation. He had talked and prepared us at three conferences during the day physically (posture and breathing) and mentally. Then in the evening he led us in a silent meditation, at least almost silent – he spoke about three times during the hour, just a sentence, to keep our thoughts in control. A few of us were carried with him on to a different level of consciousness. When the hour was up, I felt it was painful for him to come out of his meditation; he bowed to us and went into a small room alone to 'recover'. I felt I would like to have gone off alone to recover also!

This was perhaps the most valuable experience of all, because it was a deliberate act of will. It did not come unasked from outside, but depended on one's own mind control. It brought with it a vision of life, a wonder of the marvels of this universe; it altered one's values. I couldn't do this for myself. It was this highly trained Sikh who somehow conveyed what he was doing to others, and carried us with him.

F. 68 (?)   2602

My father died in a mental home. He died believing God did not care. Afterwards I felt very bitter. I could not go to church. Mother was in bed, a semi-invalid. One night I was in bed – *I was NOT asleep* – Mother was in bed with me. I was feeling very miserable. God did not care.

Someone came through the door – I just saw a form, but no details. A voice said, 'What is the matter?' I said God didn't care. Then the voice said, 'Don't you remember *I thought* I was alone and forsaken?' – and He stood just another minute and then was gone. I remembered how He had cried 'My God, my God, why hast Thou forsaken me?' Such a different feeling came over me then.

That was the only night my Mother slept well without pain.

When in Wales I liked to go to the Sunday evening service in a little village. There was a short cut up a dark lane. One Sunday evening it was specially dark and I did not like going down the lane on the return walk. I waited, hoping someone else would be going that way. No one came. I tried to be brave – I'd be home so much sooner. I told myself perhaps God would let an angel be with me. I started. Almost immediately a big black dog came cuddling up to my side and walked with me every step of the way, through our gate to the front door, and then he just went. I never saw him before or since.

F ? (eight years ago, six years ago) 4545

After a hard day at the office, I arrived home feeling completely exhausted and felt ill all that evening, also knowing I had to get up next morning to attend a three-day course, and quite frankly did not think I would be able to go. I got into bed and muttered something about 'Will somebody please help me?' I had my one arm over my head partially covering my eyes, when I suddenly thought 'What's happening? It's getting lighter.' Removing my arm, I saw from the corner of my bedroom by the ceiling a light. This got brighter and brighter and expanded to about the size of a dinner plate, then suddenly rays of light came towards me and by now its colour was a beautiful silvery white (I cannot describe it as any other colour; it really was out of this world). I must have then gone into a very deep sleep, for the next thing I remember it was morning and I felt wonderful, except for a feeling of sadness that I could not see the silvery white light again. Needless to say, I have never forgotten it and was able to attend my three-day course. I do firmly believe it was some kind of healing power. This happened about eight years ago.

Another experience was when I attended a church service. The service and sermon seemed to go on and on, when I saw a shadowy figure on the wall at the back of the platform. It was getting clearer (normally I would have dismissed it). I could not take my eyes away from it. Suddenly it came off the wall and to me materialized. She was a lady of indescribable beauty, peace and tranquillity. By this time she was standing by the front row and then she disappeared. No one else had seen her and, to be quite frank, I think I was considered to be a little bit off my head. Is it any wonder we don't talk about these things?

I have never forgotten this beautiful spiritual Being, and mentally she kept coming back to me quite frequently for twelve months afterwards. Then the man who had taken the service came back again, so I went for a sitting with him, intending to tell him about all this. As I walked into the room (he was a psychic artist) he started drawing and when he had finished, he handed me 'my Lady's' picture – and this was twelve months after I had actually seen her, so I told him what had happened. Her picture is now kept in my bedroom and I would never part with it.

M. 62 (32)   **Unnumbered**

I had gone for a long walk through Hyde Park and over to Bond
Street, where I then went into an art gallery unknown to me. There
was an exhibition of Salvador Dali's jewellery. Two pieces of this
exhibition drew my attention more than the others. One was a plain
gold frame of a cross in which you could see through, alongside or
behind it, a cluster of rubies shaped like a heart. That (heart)
appeared to be pulsating. I remember standing looking at this
pulsating heart, but for how long I do not know. I do not remember
leaving the exhibition nor how I got home. Next thing I am aware
of, I am lying on my bed enveloped in a golden glow. I felt I was in
another dimension, wrapped in a warmth, with the sense of being
united to the all of everything. I was part of everything, and all of
creation. There was a great sense of oneness, of being loved into
creation's activity.

M. ? (sixteen years ago)   **2676**

I would say that I have had three types of experience, all of which
took place during a period of some stress some sixteen years ago.

Briefly, the first one occurred shortly before the death of my
wife, when, during a 'laying on of the hands' ceremony conducted
at home by a priest – a complete stranger – I felt distinctly a fourth
presence in the room and 'saw' in my mind a huge figure behind
me, which I knew to be Jesus. (At this time I was an agnostic and
very bitter about religious establishments.)

Then, perhaps two weeks after my wife's death, during the
intercessions period of a church service, when deep in silent prayer,
I suddenly became aware that I was enshrouded by a sort of
nebulous cocoon – something like a cloud – and when this
disappeared, found that the rest of the congregation were up and
singing the final hymn. A most glorious feeling of warmth and well-
being resulted from this experience, which occurred twice more –
once at work, when walking through a very large and busy factory
with my mind fully occupied on my job, perhaps a fortnight or so
after the first one; and then again a month later, when returning
home on a bus and feeling rather 'drained' after a busy day.

Similar in type but different in application was a series of six or seven experiences, all during church services, which began a few weeks after my wife's death, when I became conscious of a particular figure in the choir – quite unknown to me – being surrounded by a sort of glow which picked her out distinctly. On later investigation I could find no window in the church fabric through which the sun, for instance, could have shone on to that area, nor were there any spot or other lights inside directed in that direction. At a much later date I found that this lady was herself going through a time of great stress, having suddenly lost her fiancé in a road accident.

The third type had its origins six months before my wife's death, when she was in hospital and expected to die at any moment. I was persuaded to allow a visiting 'faith healer' to see her. This had to be done privately, unknown about even to the hospital staff. His first words on entering the room were 'Hello, E, you look so wonderful as I see you, soon, on a hillside picking spring flowers and dancing in the joy of spring.' In fact, a remarkable recovery occurred, but this declined later and she died in July of that year. Some three months after her death a man, a complete stranger to me, came to my office and said that he had a message for me, which he didn't understand but which he had been bidden to impart, that on my next visit to church I was to fill my mind with thoughts of a green hillside and spring flowers.

Since then I have again become disillusioned with the doctrinal Church; have indeed left it; but these experiences have given me a complete faith in the continuing life of the spirit after bodily death, and perhaps this is what it was all about.

F. ? (?)   44⁶5

I have had many spiritual experiences but rarely talk about them because people regard you as 'slightly peculiar' or you 'give them the shivers'; or they devalue the experience by diminishing it and trying to find plausible explanations. Also, the experience may have been so profound that one does not wish to talk about it.

When I was in my early teens, I set myself a task, a personal quest to find out if God existed or not. I was prepared for this to take a long time, but I felt I could not be a 'don't know' and if God did exist, he must be capable of being found.

About a year later while walking home one dark night I reflected how my search was going and, rather sadly, felt that, like Thomas, I must have proof and without that I would have to say that I did not believe in a God. Deep in thought, I looked up at the night sky, which was filled with hundreds of stars. Wildly, I threw the silent call upwards, 'Prove it!' Hardly had the words been formed than a bright star sped across the sky. Before it died away, another star had begun to traverse the darkness. And there, just for a moment, an enormous cross blazed in the heavens like a personal signature. I was filled with awe and a certain terror at the power that I saw unleashed.

Thinking about it afterwards was just as mind-boggling. That the planets that had burnt out many years before should answer a personal question. Had God already anticipated my search and, therefore, my question at that moment? Such a plan was beyond human comprehension.

The knowledge of God came three years later while attending a youth camp run by Franciscan monks. A piece of driftwood in the shape of a cross was stuck in the sand dunes and every morning a few people would collect around this for communion.

One morning when I attended, it was particularly windy. The sacred wafers were snatched from our hands and blown with gay abandon across the sand. Giggling, we received the wafers a second time. As we stood at the end of the service, I looked out across the bay. It was a beautiful morning. A ray of sun broke through the cloud and streamed down on to the water and as it touched the sea, it was as if I saw the white gleaming figure of Christ. He stood on the sea as if it were solid land. So far away and yet, in that moment, so near I could have put out my hand and touched him. Then I was filled up. That is the only word I can use to describe it. I felt I was being filled up, something being poured into me as into an empty vessel, and then I knew there was a God. There was no need any more to have faith or to believe, for now I knew God as a fact, a knowledge as certain as I am here and you are there.

My husband died last year at the age of 39 years with cancer. While I nursed him a friend said to me, 'I don't know how you can believe in God.' The question surprised me, for once you know there is a God, the question of belief ceases to exist. The theological arguments, the different faiths all fade into insignificance before this fact.

Since those first spiritual experiences I have had many more. I feel they have added an extra dimension and depth to my life that would not have been there otherwise. I accept the experiences as gifts. I can never make them happen, and feel they come *to me* and not *from me*. They produce in me feelings of awe, reverence, humility, submission, peace and love. They bring with them feelings of love, compassion, strength, power and control.

F. ? (thirty years ago, fourteen years ago)   4521

Having returned from hospital after a nervous breakdown, I was back home looking after my ageing parents. Seeing so many mundane things that needed to be done, I began undertaking the various tasks, although still completely drained of energy, when suddenly I felt an extraordinary feeling and surge of strength rising up through my body, an unseen force permeating all my being, and from that moment I regained my powers of energy and vitality. I told no one, but was extremely grateful to God.

Another time the most sublime ten minutes, nature at its best. In America on holiday I was running down a steep bank through huge pine trees and landed at the foot of a little stream bathed in sunshine, surrounded with flowers. I became hypnotized and enchanted, and found myself communing with God and feeling a close presence. Whenever I recall the occasion, it leaves me full of peace.

These two encounters have given me two timeless moments of the feeling of an undeniable presence.

F. ? (14, and three and a half years ago)   4555

My first experience was at 14. I was sitting in a silent Quaker meeting. I do not remember what I was thinking. I became conscious of a quite physical Presence standing beside me, urging me to give my life to His direction in exchange for His guidance and friendship. I cannot say I heard a voice but I knew the words that had been 'said'. It remains as real to me today as at that moment, and the recollection of the promise has upheld me all the way.

The other experience I will try to recount was not particularly the presence of God. I was ill, having had an internal haemorrhage not diagnosed until a crisis. After a semi-conscious night, the consultant surgeon was summoned and ordered immediate operation. As I was wheeled into the anteroom, I heard the attendant say 'Tell him to hurry, she won't last long', obviously thinking me unconscious.

Almost at once, it seemed to me, I was in the presence of 'people', who came towards me with great joy and welcome, holding out their arms to greet me, wanting to embrace and take me with them to others they indicated were waiting for me. I could not describe their bodies or clothes, but they had substance of some kind; they did not use words I could remember later, but I knew what they said to me, and their joy surrounded me. I began to protest in anguish that I must go back – as clearly as if today I hear myself explaining, 'I *must* go back, I am so sorry, but I *must* . . . R [my husband] can't manage the boys and the church and everything without me; I have to go back because they need me so . . .' As I protested more and more, their joy turned to just gentleness and they gradually faded backwards.

It all lasted only a few moments it seemed. I remember nothing more until late the next day when efforts were being made to rouse me. The day after that the houseman came and sat by my bed. 'Phew! Am I glad to see you alive!' he said. I made some jocular comment about being rather pleased myself, and he replied soberly: 'But, you see, I have to confess that I did not believe your GP's diagnosis of extremely urgent haemorrhage and I would not have the consultant surgeon woken until it was nearly too late, and consequently your heart stopped as we took you in to surgery, and for some moments you were dead.'

It is perhaps worth adding that (a) the doctor agreed the experience I described must have been during the period I was 'dead' because of timing, and (b) while this experience was taking place my husband knelt in a nearby empty church praying desperately I should not die.

F. ? (twenty years ago) 4764

1. My husband, children and I were visiting Y National Park. We had stopped to eat a picnic lunch beside a rushing stream. After lunch, my husband was busy checking out something on the car and the children had gone off to play. I found myself alone and started climbing around on some rocks out into the centre of the stream. I sat down on one of the rocks and became fascinated with the ripples on the surface of the water and the way they were sparkling in the sun. Then, it was as though time stood still. I don't know how long I sat there and stared at what now looked like thousands of sparkling lights. I lost all consciousness of anything else in my surroundings. Later, as I drifted back into my usual consciousness, I was thinking that our whole world is a reflection of many aspects of some great oneness that includes everything that is.

2. Sometimes when I am at the beach, looking out over the ocean, I think about the other side, far across the ocean. One day my thoughts took a different direction and I became conscious of a more distant shore, much more distant than anything on Earth, over some vast expanse of space. It seemed very personal to me, as if I had some close connection with it, like it was another home, with people I loved and from whom I was now separated. I think of this every once in a while and wonder if I will ever get back there. Also, I wonder if others have had a similar experience.

3. One afternoon while I was at home alone, just relaxing, I started thinking about the universe, how big it must be, perhaps never ending. I was wondering about that. How could something never end? Suddenly, it was as if a funnel was in the top of my head and my consciousness went out into it, spreading wider and wider as it went. This went on for quite some time until I suddenly realized that I was conscious of everything that is, and that I was part of it all. Then I became aware of it from a different aspect. I was everything that is. It seemed curious at first, but then turned into a feeling of being very much alone. I thought surely there must be something or somebody outside of me, but I searched and searched and could find nothing that was not a part of me. Desperately, I wanted someone to share my existence. Finally, the loneliness became overwhelming and I snapped back into my usual

little self. This was experienced almost twenty years ago but I have never forgotten it. It changed my life, giving me a strong feeling of empathy for all the people around me and even all those I have never met. We are all in the same boat.

M. ? (?) 4744

I'd been in bed a couple of days with a cold. That night faces appeared at the bedroom window, the light bulb began to glow and there was a figure on it.

I finally fell asleep. The next morning I awoke at dawn. My eyes went straight to the wardrobe: there were two faces on it. One was the face of Christ, the other the eyes followed (just like some photos) wherever I moved; I had the idea this was a woman.

Then I was asked if I was willing to die to be a soldier of Jesus Christ. It wasn't a voice; it came like a thought. I said I was and I was told to look up into the sky. I saw a chariot, the angel of God was in it. This was followed by a cross, as bright as the sun; it filled the whole of the sky. The next thing I was lying in the bottom of a grave; it was open. I came up out of it as though I was floating. I looked down and saw a coffin gleaming with light.

The next few days I didn't want to eat, I wanted nothing. We talked about quite a few things. I know he has a sense of humour; he told me the heart is just a brass pump, it has nothing to do with life.

No one believed me. I've been written off twice since then (according to doctors). Once I was supposed to have a coronary. I went into hospital, a lady put one of those machines on me, she just tore up the paper that was coming out of it and walked away. She thought it was a waste of time. Then I had pernicious anaemia. 'It can't be cured', they said. 'You will have to have jabs for the rest of your life.' I swear by Almighty God I have not had any injections; for many years I've had no trouble with it since.

M. 25 (19) 583

I have always been interested in analysing my experience of the universe. Some experiences, however, stand out in my memory as being more intense, more real, than others.

One of these experiences happened when I was 19. I had been on holiday in Scotland on my own for a week. Earlier in the week I had caught a glimpse of a buzzard flying over a loch and, being particularly interested in birds of prey (my interest is more aesthetic than anything else), I hoped to see some more. I was unsuccessful until about four o'clock on the following Friday afternoon. I had been walking more or less aimlessly all day, it was very hot and the streams were drying up so that I was continually thirsty. The ground I covered was very steep and tiring, my feet were blistered and I had not eaten since 10 a.m. All in all I was completely exhausted and having one disappointment after another. I kept straining my eyes at every large bird I saw on the horizon, but no buzzards. I think that the birds of prey are, to me, a symbol of a projection, of a deep wish to be totally free. I suspect that we all know this freedom as children but it is so delicate that it can easily be lost as we get older. I think all great art, music, painting, literature, and feats of courage and endurance remind us of this feeling of unlimitedness of childhood, and the more this feeling is able to manifest itself consciously the more sensitive we are to these things. Birds of prey, then, can do for me what the music of Beethoven can do for others.

Although it was unreasonable, I felt as though something was compelling me to go on looking, but by four o'clock I was sick of the hills, the heather, the trees, the sun and everything under it. I decided to return to my campsite and start packing for my return home the next morning. I felt as though my holiday had been a complete waste of time; I was more tired than when I had come and the only prospect I had was going back to the routine of life until my next holiday came round. I can't express how dejected I felt as I walked (limped) back. Everything seemed pointless, including myself. I seemed to be lost in a whirlpool of thoughts that went round and round; all questions and no answers.

I was completely oblivious of my surroundings and walked automatically as if in a trance. Then I heard a sound behind me that I had never heard before and when I turned round to investigate, I saw four buzzards directly overhead. I felt as if they had called to let me know they were there. From the moment I turned I felt all the fatigue drop away, all the pessimism and anxieties. The feeling of being narrow and cut off from something became a feeling of being vast and unbounded, as if I was connected with the whole universe. I understood William Blake's poem 'To see a world in a grain of sand'. Everything, including the stones on the path, seemed to be infinitely significant. As I watched the buzzards spiralling in the blue sky I felt identified with them and yet at the same time I was intensely aware of my own identity. I felt as though I were the centre of the universe and at the same time the centre was everywhere. I was conscious of a sustained power and the buzzards seemed to be a manifestation of it; they moved without effort and they had a wide field of vision up there. They were a reflection of everything I was feeling surging through me at that moment.

I lifted my binoculars to watch them but I felt irritation at this; I wanted to remain completely passive and let the whole of the scene rush in on me. I felt as if a filter had been taken from my senses and I was seeing the concrete world as it really is and the purpose and meaning of it all. Time was suspended; I watched the buzzards until they were out of sight but I have no idea of how long it was. After I lost sight of the birds, I literally skipped down the path on my way home. That one short experience gave significance to the week and everything that had led up to it. There was harmony where there had been disharmony. I felt as if I had been given a gift from the gods.

This experience seemed so paradoxical and so meaningful that I have reflected on it over and over again, and I realize it was only a more intense, more qualitative form of similar experiences I have had. During these years I have been to both psychological extremes of near-insanity or chaos to one of certainty that the chaos can be overcome and that there is a purpose in the universe, of which man is the spearhead.

I got to the point two years ago where I was ready to enter a mental hospital and either get 'cured' or escape into insanity until I was dead. Fortunately, I heard about Maharishi Mahesh Yogi insisting that it was easy to tap the 'source of power, meaning and purpose' inside oneself. I had nothing to lose and I decided to give it a try. At least, I thought, if I can aim for that state of consciousness and reach it, I will know that it is not hallucination and that it can be induced purposefully instead of by accident. After three days of practising meditation for two periods a day of a half hour each period, I attained the 'peak experience' of my life.

From the beginning of my meditation I could feel an increase in energy and clarity of mind. When I experienced this transcending of thought, I felt again what I had felt in Scotland: unbounded, in harmony with the universe, decisive, clear, patient, serene, godlike. I felt as though I were being swept into an unbounded ocean of energy and all I had to do was let myself be carried by it. I was conscious of a vast light that radiated from nowhere, not a dazzling light but soft like a pastel shade. I was intensely aware of my body, my breathing and heartbeat, and again I felt at the centre of everything, but with a profound sense of humility. I could hear my bedroom clock ticking but it wasn't associated with time, just the sound of the mechanism was infinitely beautiful for its own sake.

Through my experiences and research I have come to believe that there is a purpose behind the universe and that it is working through the laws of evolution, the purpose being the extension of consciousness, understanding, and sensitivity, and that man is capable of uncovering this purpose through his understanding of the mechanism of the mind.

M. 60 (19, 22) 3144

Two particular experiences are selected for recording here because, though different in kind, both seemed to me to be of a religious nature and both made a specially vivid impression on my mind.

The first was, I think, in the early spring. I was in the garden of my parents' home and aged 19 at the time. I was standing near the trunk of an oak tree, looking down at a bank and the fresh green leaves of wild violets and other small plants on the ground. I was experiencing thoughts of joy and love towards all the small and great manifestations of nature around me in that quiet place. As I watched, there was quite quickly a silent change. I looked with astonishment at the leaves and blades of grass. They had taken on what appeared to be an internal light of their own. They shone with a quiet radiance, and so did everything within my field of vision. I stood dead still, not daring to move. I felt tremendously uplifted and thankful as I watched this extraordinary living light, which seemed also to have gentle sounds associated with it. It was as if I could hear the leaves growing. I noticed that all the colours were enhanced and brighter and more alive than normal. The impression received was that I was looking at something real and fundamental and not just imagined by me. I do not know whether it lasted for seconds or minutes before, equally without warning, everything quietly returned to the relative dullness of its material exterior.

The second event occurred in Persia at an altitude of about 10,000 feet in the mountains. The scenery was extremely dramatic. I was walking, followed by a Persian tribesman, along a scree parallel to, and at a reasonably safe distance from, the top of a vast cliff that dropped for an unknown depth into a chasm below me on my right. Across the far side of this chasm was an impressive mass of spires of rock reaching into the sky that inevitably made one think of a cathedral, so much so that my companions in our camp and I always referred to these rocks as the cathedral rocks.

The air and the light were exhilarating. Visibility was more than 100 miles. As I walked along I came opposite a huge V-shaped cleft in the rocks on the far side of the ravine that separated me from those rocks, and near the centre of the ravine was a natural rough platform of rock. Suddenly I had the strong impression of a huge figure, which I estimated to be about sixty feet high and composed of living radiating light, apparently standing on, or just above, this platform. Again I felt tremendously uplifted and happy, and at peace with all created things. The Being seemed to be aware of my presence, but only incidentally, and I had the feeling that he/ she was conscious of everything existing within a very large radius all around. I stood still, again for a period of time of which I have no clear recollection. After a while I noticed the Persian tribesman staring not at the platform of rock, but at me, and I thought it was time to move on. It was several days before the feeling of upliftment and expansion of consciousness had entirely worn off.

F. 86 (74, 83) 4103

After the sudden death of my husband twelve years ago, I decided to look into contemplative meditation. I live alone, so can find the necessary quietness, and have indeed benefited enormously in that and have found a spiritual awareness, which has completely changed my life. I am wondering if this can have resulted in the two experiences I have had.

My first experience took place one lovely sunny morning on a tree-lined road. Suddenly, the colour of the sky, the trees and flowers intensified in colour, I felt real life surging in the tree trunks and seemed to be lifted up almost to another dimension. I felt I was myself part of something immense. I also felt I had found a deeper meaning to life. Then it faded and returned to normal again.

My second experience, some three years ago, came in a dream in which I was with someone who had an affectionate arm across my shoulder. Then a most beautiful screen of orange flames appeared in front of me. I expressed my delight, then I felt a warm brush on my left cheek and that was immediately followed by what I can only describe as an '*explosion*' of intensely brilliant light, which filled my body. I shot my feet out of bed (it was 2.30 a.m.) and sat on the bedside holding my arms around my chest in ecstasy of this intense light. It was some time before it faded, but even that day it didn't really leave me, and for many days it was still within me. The bliss and ecstasy the experience gave me I cannot find words to describe and I have had no further experiences since.

F. 65 (?) 4063

My husband was in Africa and in those days we numbered our letters to each other as so many were lost in transit.

On this particular evening I had gone to bed and was not unduly concerned, as my husband's letters were fairly frequent. After my usual prayers, I fell asleep. Suddenly something had awakened me. I could feel a presence in the room. As I turned over, there, a few inches from my face, was the head and shoulders of my husband, so lifelike I could not believe it and, yes! I was frightened too.

Something compelled me to look at him. As I turned, so whatever it was followed, still a few inches from my face. Then, as suddenly as it had happened, it disappeared, leaving a feeling of emptiness in the room.

Immediately I got up and wrote a letter to my husband, stating time and date. Our letters crossed in the post and my husband said he'd nearly been killed and in those few moments he prayed to come home safely, and the time, as you can guess, was when I saw him.

I saw nothing again until a few years ago, when my husband was taking a late bath. Again I was in bed when something awakened me. Kneeling by the bed was, as I thought, my husband. When I spoke to him and got no reply, I just knew it had happened again. Luckily, we do not lock our bathroom door, as my husband was sound asleep in a freezing cold bath, just a few inches from going under the water.

I just cannot understand it, as he appears before me so real, not a bit ghostly or anything like that.

At times I can sense when something is going to happen, but I see nothing at these times, just have that feeling that some incident will occur.

F. ? (?)   2547

Since the death of my son a year ago I have had a sort of volcanic eruption of mystical experiences, including becoming clairaudient. I have tried twice to write these experiences, but have not been able to, I suppose, face their implications on paper.

My son was a pharmacologist. His PhD thesis, which I typed from his dictation, was about malaria. As I typed it, as we did with all his work, we played a sort of game. I told him the first word or two of the next phrase, and usually it was correct. When he was a child he sometimes repeated aloud names and phrases that I was thinking, even a complicated Dutch name.

After he died, six months afterwards, I suddenly became able to converse with him; his voice 'appeared' in my head. Immediately after his death, a fortnight later, I had an experience of complete numinous knowledge of his presence. Until then, though a mystical

Quaker, I had not been able to make up my mind about personal survival of death. After G started to talk to me, I suppose my balance was temporarily lost. I went through what I think the psalmist might have meant by the valley of the shadow, being made to examine all sorts of concepts of which I had previously been only dimly aware, if at all. I'm a painter and handweaver and spinner, and completely ignorant of theology.

A doctor friend arranged for me to talk to a psychiatrist, who, I discovered later, has written several books on subjects relating to the experiences I have. He said that I am as sane as he is, that in his opinion God was communicating with me, as I knew – though, of course, I was alarmed lest I should be psychotic under the stress of grief – and that I should go ahead and do my best.

Under my son's guidance I started to practise a form of contemplative prayer, which later I found described in various mystical works, including St Theresa and the *Cloud of Unknowing*. I have always been accustomed to pray at nights for healing, and in the past year people really have been healed. At first I laid on hands, but later discovered that it works just as well while meditating and the subject doesn't even need to know, which is really better, especially with people who wouldn't accept the possibility of such a thing, until afterwards, when relieved of long-standing pain.

My own body is changing too; I have always had one hip higher than the other due to an old injury as a baby, which makes (made) one leg about an inch and a half shorter than the other. I've had treatment for this, and limped. Now my two legs are the same length. Also I no longer feel pain, when I burn myself on the oven, for instance.

And there are other manifestations. I have twice visited an old lady who has been bedridden in a nursing home for five years, while lying on my bed in meditation. She has received these visits. I couldn't believe at first that this was not my imagination, but it seemed so real, I could feel her voice in my throat, and the next day I went to see her, but when I got there, it seemed so strange, I could not ask. However, she said, 'P, dear, you came to see me yesterday, but a nurse and some 'real' visitors said I must be going senile as there was nobody here.'

Since then I have been prompted to visit and comfort people

who are in some way incarcerated, whom I don't know, so, of course, I do not know if they receive the visits. I think it is only people cut off from the normal sensory stimuli who can perceive this phenomenon, and usually when they are especially sad. It is quite easy for me to do it.

I have always had a very scrupulous regard for truth and for being objective, as far as one can. The change in myself is profound; I exist to do what God wants, as far as I can. As St Theresa said, God has no eyes to see with but mine, and, in the same way, what each of us can contribute is special, and together we are weaving a pattern, which must somehow be specially vital now, with our society so badly astray (some of my visions have been apocalyptic).

I have started to read Jung's works, and much that he says is relevant: what he says about the individuation process, and his essay on acausal synchronicity and about archetypes. And he himself obviously had similar visions and experiences – he mentions in his autobiography feeling the voice in his throat and tongue, which I do when somebody else speaks. This really is a comfort. I'm a sane and normal, motherly person. I have never had any kind of mental treatment and now have to accept that God is taking this way of developing in me latent qualities which I really have known about since early childhood, but was, I suppose, too lazy to pursue without a great deal of stimulus – so it had to be done in this very violent way.

F. ? (?)   4496

From being a child I have had several odd experiences, from distinctly hearing a voice to seeing people I subsequently found had passed over some time ago. Sadly, I ignored all of this, and in fact was rather scared until six years ago I had a baby who lived only a week. For several months I was depressed and searched for a meaning to this. I visited a spiritualist open circle for the first time and was told, among other confirmatory things, that the baby was only temporarily 'in spirit'. This encouraged me to try again and I had another, perfect baby, five years ago. That spiritualist message stunned me at the time and I was very emotional. It did, however, change my life, as I was afraid of having another child.

Since then I have investigated spiritualism, learned what I can, tried, unsuccessfully, to develop clairvoyance, but have experienced feelings of pure ecstasy – a sort of holy feeling – several times in meditation. I can only describe it as feeling wrapped in light which you know you belong to. Also during these meditations I felt from the beginning a sort of tingling or extremely light pressure around my head, my arms were lifted and face seemed to mould itself into different faces several times. I would like to tell of two dreams.

In the first I was walking along a valley bordered by cliffs when there was an earthquake and rocks began to fall upon me. I realized I was about to be buried by the falling rocks and was appalled, as I hate being closed in. Suddenly 'I' shot out of my body through the top of my head – quite easily. I remember being so relieved to be out of the physical body and amazed at how easy I had gotten out!

In the second dream I was climbing up a rather steep hill/cliff, carrying my mother on my back. At the top was a sort of monastery which I knew I had to reach. I kept stumbling but eventually came near and had doubts whether I was going to manage the final yard or so. Then a hand reached down and held mine and there shot through my body such a feeling of love, compassion, understanding and energy that I was moved to tears but bodily lifted, with my mother, into the holy place. I never saw who it was that lifted me but the feeling was so spiritual, I felt touched by the 'Holy Spirit' and have never forgotten.

I know that I am part of that, somehow, and it is such a comfort.

M. ? (?)   1145

Having finished my secondary studies with very good results in physics, chemistry and biology, I got the advice to study science. Personally, I felt more like becoming an engineer and the family tradition was rather in the direction of the law and of public administration. All this rather bewildered me, but I would not say that I was in a state of acute crisis. Anyhow, I prayed God for guidance what to choose.

One night I woke up and it was as though a voice said: 'Your task is to work for the conciliation of nations.' The message was quite clear and I knew I was not dreaming. I cannot say I actually heard a voice with my ears. It was rather as though I knew someone spoke to me. Having heard the message, I straightaway went off to sleep again.

This vision was one of the reasons for me to start studying law, though at the time I rationalized my choice with the argument that I did not feel strong enough in mathematics for a career in science.

Later on in my life I sometimes tried to deviate from the path I had been shown, but I was brought back on the rails every time again. The curious thing is that I can say with hindsight that most of my deviations really were nothing but preparations for later work. One of the deviations was to think of joining a colonial administration. My interest in these questions later came very handy when dealing with questions of developing countries. Other temporary interests from the main course proved equally useful.

Now I am an ambassador, to be retired in a few years. I cannot boast any great successes and I leave it to God to judge if I have been true to His voice and if I used the talents He gave me to His satisfaction. One thing I am certain of is that the voice was true.

As I suppose it is the character of the experience that interests you most of all, I would like to mention to you that I had three experiences that in their character were very similar as far as the form was concerned. The interesting thing is that these visions can be checked and proved correct.

The first case was that of a mutiny that preoccupied me very much. In this case I also woke up during the night and it was as though I was looking at the scene through binoculars. The field of vision was small. I distinctly saw the scene and I saw the smoke of an explosion. Then I knew that the matter had been settled. As I was anxious to check what I had seen, I looked at my watch, noted the time on a piece of paper and went off to sleep again.

This was in the days before broadcasting, so I could not have known what had happened when I told my parents the next morning that at such and such a time the whole of the drama had been over. Later on it was published that the mutiny had in effect been ended by the explosion of a bomb at the time I had noted. I do not think this experience by itself is very special. Such visions seem to be pretty frequent, though they are probably more common in primitive countries where people's minds are less trained always to be focused on actual situations than in our so-called advanced countries.

The second case is a vision that, to me, has always seemed stranger. Again I woke up at night and I saw the apostle Paul being led away by the Roman soldiers into the fortress in Jerusalem and turning to the mass of people that had tried to murder him to make his speech that is reported in Acts 22. I did not actually perceive what he really said. It was just a kind of short film and I was among the onlookers. It was a vision that in no way corresponded to what I had pictured myself that happened when reading the Bible. The apostle was just an ugly little Jew. The fortress was very different from what I had imagined it to be. Moreover, I had never been especially touched by this scene. The scene of the apostle taking leave of the elders of Ephesus, for instance, has always been far more moving to me. So I cannot explain emotionally why I had this vision. But the curious thing is that years later I saw a reconstruction of the fortress according to recent excavations and there was the fortress of my vision. Still later, I read somewhere of a tradition that Saint Paul had been a small, very unimpressive man but that his eyes and his voice gave him great power. This tradition was absolutely in accordance with my vision.

These visions have in common their mechanism. They were no dreams. The perception was absolutely clear and definite.

F. 75 (70)   4185

I made a commitment to Christ when I was 22, but after many years of unsatisfactory discipleship I fell away, ceasing to attend church, read the Bible and pray, declaring myself an agnostic.

When I was turned 70, I attended a course of T. S. Eliot's poetry, and study of the 'Four Quartets', combined with other factors, brought me back to faith. So soon as I had made this fresh commitment I had three experiences, which are, I believe, relatively common ones but which strengthened my faith very greatly. Firstly, for several months, I was deeply conscious of being loved and experienced a strange warmth. One uses the expression 'heart-warming' but this warmth extended over my body and was not attributable to anything physical and felt especially when I was resting in bed. Secondly, when I prayed, I had the impression that the sun was shining brightly and sometimes was surprised on opening my eyes to find the day dull and cloudy. Thirdly, and I think this happened once only, when praying for individuals, I saw in my mind's eye shafts of light directed downwards in various directions, as if they were illuminating those for whom I was praying. It was like wartime searchlight display in reverse, coming from above instead of ground-level.

This renewal happened about five years ago, since when I have known almost unclouded love, joy and peace.

F. 19 (?)   4127

I am a girl of 19 years old, I have my own business and consider myself to be very lucky indeed. Sometimes too lucky. I always knew where and how I wanted to be and, although I was at times very hard to live with, I meant well – I kept in touch with God and I genuinely felt pain when I sinned against him. I committed petty crimes and consistently asked for God's forgiveness. I developed many areas of my subconscious and believed in what I was doing – I knew there was something to be found. But in my private investigation, which started when I was about 13 years old, I found drugs useful and I smoked and injected and carried on discovering about my subconscious and my connections to God. For years, though, God had hinted at his existence. I prayed every day – sometimes to say a Hail Mary during the course of my day was a habitual act which I found I used in all types of circum-stances. I never really shared my belief in God – I wasn't even sure which religion I was perturbing [sic] towards; I had a Jewish father and Christian mother and had a small time at a Catholic school.

I went through a period between 15 and 18 years in which I discovered a lot, especially with people and psychologically, but at the same time I was taking too many drugs. I went to Spain for three months, continued to take drugs and turned what I had learnt about people upon myself. I began to drive myself into a wholly messy situation; I was mixed up and very frightened.

I went into hospital for an overdose and during that stay I had the most incredible experience I ever had. Every day from my hospital bed I could see a beautiful tree, which the sun would set behind in the evening, and in the distance the top of the spire of the cathedral. The tree was my stimulant back to health. I continuously prayed for forgiveness to God and with the powers I had discovered I would try to calm the baby which persistently cried in the room next door each night – with the power of God I found I could.

One day I had a telephone call. After it, I suddenly felt this incredible feeling of exaltation. I fell on to my knees by the window, with tears pouring down my face, praising God.

I felt incredible, a totally new person. It has changed my life, but to start saying how could take more pages than I have time to write.

F. ? (?)   4232

I have decided to write about one or two of my own experiences in the hope that they may be of help. (Also for quite a selfish reason, in that it will be quite a relief to tell someone!) Before I go on further, however, I ought to state that I'm not a religious person at all. Nevertheless, these past few years I have become quite convinced that there is some sort of spiritual existence and some sort of life after death. I'll now try to tell you of the unrelated experiences which have, together, I think, led me to believe this.

Firstly, quite non-psychic experiences. However down in the dumps I might feel at the time, I can suddenly and unexpectedly feel intense elation and an extraordinary sense of the beauty and unity of all life when looking at our quite ordinary garden – the stones, plants, trees, etc. Of course, on most occasions it looks just like the rather untidy garden that it is!

My husband always says, when all is going wrong, that there is always 'the wind on the heath'. I never understood this at all until I had such experiences. It is quite difficult to explain how out of the ordinary they are, yet they are definitely quite different from normal types of experience and alter one's view of life.

Two other experiences have also led me to feel that people do not die altogether, as it were. Firstly, the day after my husband's father had died I definitely felt his presence in the room – no visions or anything but a comforting all-pervading calm. So there was no case of fear or of ghostly manifestations.

The second experience occurred at a time when I was in a very depressed state, full of despair. As a child I was extremely close to an uncle who, sadly, died. One night, when the depression had sort of reached a crescendo (if that is the word), I began to think of this uncle and wondered why dead people seem to have no contact with the living at all however close their relationship. Suddenly I was aware of my uncle (again not visually) and again through a tremendous all-pervading calm, which in my, at that time, constant state of agitation and so on was like a miracle. And the state of calm lasted a long time.

Two other experiences were rather more disturbing to me – both experiences to do with relatives who were gravely ill. I had better add that I did not feel emotionally close to either of them.

One morning we were told that my mother-in-law had suddenly become ill and was not expected to live many hours. When I retired to bed, she was still alive. I could not sleep and in the early hours of the morning a very bright light appeared in my head (my eyes were closed and the room was dark). It stayed for a short time and then, quite abruptly, went out. At that I just knew without a doubt that my mother-in-law had died and next morning we were informed that she had died in the early hours of the morning.

Again, I was informed that an uncle had been taken to hospital gravely ill. One night two or three weeks later I could not sleep. The hours passed by and I became increasingly distressed through a steadily increasing sort of mental torture – I cannot give it any other description and I have never experienced it before or since. It was utterly terrible. The strange thing was that while this was happening I knew quite definitely that my uncle was in terrible distress – I felt that he was dying and could not/would not die or that he was in some dreadful mental turmoil. Eventually I grew very angry, got up and, like a demented thing, began railing at God or whoever/whatever for being so unmerciful. I remember then praying to God with all the force that I could muster, begging him to be merciful, to do what was right, be it to make my uncle well or to let him die in peace. But to do it right speedily! I then felt an unutterable calm and a desire, at last, to sleep. It was actually very uncanny, but I returned to bed knowing that it had all been resolved, that my uncle had, in fact, at last died and all was well.

We were woken by a phone call the same morning to say that he had died in the early hours of that morning. Since then I have wished that I could have asked how he died – what his condition was, was he very restless and disturbed or what – but I dare not ask such questions of his widow.

I feel that I have been unable to fully express the sheer force of the experiences described in this letter. The final one was very frightening and I dread a similar experience occurring.

The two main factors which set such experiences apart from everyday life experiences are (a) the strength of feeling involved and (b) the certainty/conviction implicit in them. I am a fairly indecisive person but when such experiences occur, I become filled with certainty. I do not believe, I *know* (e.g., I *knew* that my uncle was distressed and I *knew* when he had died). As time passes I begin to doubt and begin to question, concluding often that it is just some trick of the mind – which, indeed, it probably is.

F. 46 (23)   4422

Some sorts of what I can only call 'religious experiences' have been coming to me at intervals all through my life, mainly in my teens and early twenties and again now in middle life. Linked with the experiences of my first thirty years and an inseparable part of them was what I can only describe as an embargo on speaking of them, stronger than an inhibition. I think I could not have told anyone about them at the time, though I was a very chatty, open ordinary girl. This has now been lifted and occasionally I have felt a definite push to tell someone in a specific context – always with beneficial result. It is only recently that I learnt that the word 'mystic' does actually mean 'mute', which was just how it felt.

I do not remember any particular spiritual experiences in childhood but as far back as I can remember I 'knew' of the existence of God: whatever gradually developing sense I had of myself as an entity was accompanied by a sense of someone other, invisible and infinitely greater than any other 'person' and different to them, a kind of all-powerful, pervasive force within the world but, far from being impersonal, was loving and beneficent, with a real interest in me. No doubt the good loving attributes owed something to my knowledge of my loving parents, but God was someone quite definitely other than and greater than them. I never used any word for this person – after all, I never needed to – but other people's use of the word God or Creator seemed to fit pretty well. I never saw or heard anything that I recall, but the knowledge was as certain as the knowledge that other people continued to exist when they left the room.

I came from a long line of deeply religious Free Church people on my mother's side, but as my parents were both agnostic and anti-Church, I don't remember religion ever being a topic of conversation at home. Apart from a few brief flirtations with Sunday schools, I did not attend church until, at 13 years old, I went to boarding school, as part of the family tradition. Services and discussion were obligatory but sensitively conducted and I think it must have been about then that it began to dawn on me, with considerable astonishment, that this 'knowledge' was not universal, and that other people were either uninterested in God, like my parents, or believed in him as a matter of faith, not knowledge. Religious doubts, in the usual sense, have never been a problem to me – I could more easily doubt my own existence than that of what I know as God. For many years this gave me an uncomfortable mixture of feeling 'special' but lonely, occasionally feeling I must be some sort of saint but more often realizing that I must be a failed one! The lines about those to whom much is given also made me distinctly uneasy as I heard others wrestling with religious doubt. My doubts were about the Church and the Christian religion, particularly where Jesus 'fitted in', and while I was intelligent enough to know it wasn't a matter of me fitting the universe into my framework, it caused a considerable struggle within me.

Other problems causing me great anguish at that time were those relating to salvation. The fact that my parents and brother and many others I loved were not Christians made me fear to lose them; in the rather rigid doctrinal framework of that time it seemed that they would not be saved. It may be of some interest that, looking back, I see that much of my natural adolescent ambivalence about separating as a person from my parents expressed itself in this struggle, and my unrecognized jealousy of Jesus ('our elder brother') seeming to come between me and God was a direct experience of my human sibling rivalry. How many of the grievous separations between Christians must have their origin in similar adolescent hang-ups!

In spite of the doubts I became convinced that God wished me to express my commitment to him in baptism, which took place when I was 16, to my great joy. My parents accepted it completely, saying that though they could not believe, they were sincerely glad that I could, and I joined my grandparents' Baptist church near my home and remained a keen attender for the next ten years.

For several years I then had experiences that I suppose could be classified as religious ecstasy. For some, I can remember in exact detail the place and time; for others, the experiences merge and I cannot date them accurately, but there must have been at least a dozen of these, at irregular intervals and bearing little apparent relationship to what else was happening in my life at the time, happy or sad. All had a profound and lasting effect on me. In these experiences time ceased to exist, but I suspect they took up very little Earth time. There would be a sensation of being drawn up through and out of myself, often in response to an instant of joy at a picture of beauty – a tree, a sunset cloud, a great cathedral. This went on to a total submerging in the person of God himself, in which all that could be felt was total worshipful joy, lasting for all eternity and yet no time at all. Coming back felt intolerable and yet somehow beautiful in itself – one could feel the experience of the unimaginable being clothed in images of light and beauty as the only way the memory could cope with the experience; these expressed it only in a very inadequate and partial way and yet even these memories are of beauty infinitely greater than anything else seen on Earth. Always afterwards I would be filled with peace and fulfilment, a sense of deep gratitude and awe, and a great yearning for God. I could never have spoken of, or even hinted at, these experiences to anyone else at this time.

The single other experience at this time was quite different and horrifically unpleasant: it was a vision of Hell. It took place when I was 23 and a final-year student. It blasted my priggish nice girl, good Christian image of myself into smithereens, from which no plaster saint image could ever be put together again. I suppressed most thoughts about it for years before I was mature enough, and recovered enough, to take it out and meditate on it fearlessly. It was, I am sure, the most formative experience of my life.

The circumstances were that I had been out for the evening with a young man. He was not a regular boy-friend, but I was aware that he cared for me rather more than I cared for him. He was considerably older than I and had at one time trained towards being a Catholic priest for some years, though never ordained. During the evening I had perpetrated some small verbal cruelty, the sort of thing that is common in everyday life and can ostensibly be laughed off as a joke. At the end of the evening he very gently rebuked me for it and left me at my gate.

For me, it was as if a cover was suddenly torn off a black chasm, or a piece of knitting was cut to unravel back to chaos. I saw my little meaningless bit of cruelty for what it was and inexorably, link by link, undoing to the bottom of my soul, every meanness, every unkindness, falsehood, hypocrisy, silliness unravelling to expose the very heart of evil itself – my heart. I did not lose sight of the fact that I was (by worldly standards) not particularly bad or cruel, but, on the contrary, a rather kind, earnest and socially concerned young woman. This made it much worse – I could not see myself as some great and splendid sinner. It was the small, sordid nastiness of me that was opening up pit after pit of blackness. The vision would not stop coming.

I began to walk in torment through the streets to the open country. With the eyes of my body I could see where I was going, but the vision in my mind was far more vivid, interpenetrating the 'real' world. I began to see how all my assumed kindness and decency was a desperate attempt to get away from this evil in myself, how every one of my virtues had a flip-side of unspeakable nastiness. This was not shown me as an abstract or intellectual idea: I was walking through a desolate swamp of stinking, stagnant water that I knew to be my own interior country. In the slime huge primeval monsters, rather like dinosaurs, were endlessly struggling with each other in deadly and perpetual enmity.

I saw that all evil can be reduced to two forms, the active and the passive. There is the evil that hates outwardly, that longs to crush and destroy everything in the universe and cannot rest while anything remains whole. There is the passive evil, which longs to suck in all that is, until its vast swollen stomach contains the whole universe. These huge paired monsters, Greed with her swollen belly, Hate with his jaws and pincers, were locked in totally unavailing battle, since it was of the very nature of evil, divided against itself, that it could never win, and the frustration and misery rose from the swamp as a torment that itself must last all eternity because of its very nature, not by any decree of judgement. And all this was me.

I must have wandered for many hours, overwhelmed, crying and wringing my hands, sometimes crawling rather than walking, retching and eventually vomiting. Part of me longed for someone – anyone – to rescue me. Part of me knew that nothing could stop the vision and that the kindliest person could be no more than an embarrassment. I remember wondering how I could ever live with myself again, but the thought of suicide was inconceivable – it would only remove the everyday world and I would find myself totally in this nightmare swamp. I did not feel I would be eternally damned; somewhere I knew God and all Angels watched over this swamp. I could see a silver light, but in that state it seemed infinitely far away and inaccessible. Eventually I found my way home (the house was empty) and slept.

I think it is interesting to note that I was physically as well as emotionally exhausted by this experience, being hardly able to walk for several days and recovering slowly as if I had had a serious illness. A friend nursed me and asked no questions. Again, I could not talk about it and though time dimmed the horror, I had to file the whole thing away for many years without thinking too much about it. It made me much more tolerant, but, I think, to some extent drove me away from the Church at that time, as I seemed to have so little in common with what I saw of other Christians. Perhaps I was unfair, but I think the Church twenty years ago was somewhat complacent and tended to keep on the surface of morality rather than disturb the depths. Also, I felt a hypocrite in the company of 'good' people after this.

For the next seven years I went about ordinary everyday life entirely. I attended churches spasmodically but was aware that my commitment was not what it had been, and the more I learnt of the world, the less I found I could respect the Church. I had no 'religious experiences' at that time and though I did not lose my love and reverence for 'God', I tended to think that such experiences must be linked with adolescence and would not come again.

My life at this time was unhappy. My husband, who I loved very much, broke down mentally and had many admissions to psychiatric hospital. My parents died within days of each other shortly after my son was born. We went abroad on holiday and our son, who was not yet 2, was killed in a road accident. The love and concern of the whole community, both Catholic and Protestant, was overwhelming, and this catastrophe finished the work of undoing my psyche that the vision of Hell had begun. Although I did not apparently break down – I 'coped' in worldly terms – I was desolate. I had nothing and no one, except God. I was nothing and no one – but God had me.

While we were still in a state of shock, just before the funeral, the Protestant pastor called, and read the Twenty-third Psalm. As the familiar words swept over me I was outside myself. I walked in a narrow valley – the valley of the shadow of death – on sharp uneven stones. It was absolutely dark but I was not afraid; the air was warm, with the scent of pine trees all around, and I could hear a little stream splashing and the pine trees stirring. I could walk quite safely and I knew no one ever need fear death, knowing what its valley of approach was like. I came out of the shadow of the trees and was not allowed to do more than look for a moment. I saw a simple countryside of hedges and meadows and my son playing by a stream too shallow to hurt even the smallest child. He was playing with the total absorption and content I knew so well, and the main thing was that I knew he was absolutely safe for ever and ever. More – I knew that nearby, though I could not see it, was a beautiful 'mansion', and when evening came One would come out and gently lead him home to be cared for.

This vision sustained me through the funeral and the return home and the difficult weeks after. I also had a number of brief experiences which I would classify among the so-called hallucinations of the bereaved, known to be very common. These would be a sense of A's presence, hearing his chuckle or feeling his hand in mine or on my cheek. Very often during these weeks I would feel I was living in the presence of God. This was glorious and uplifting, but at the same time frightening; I was out of my depth and had a sense of being in a world whose atmosphere I could not breathe. I feel that the death of someone so intimately a part of me as my little son had drawn me into a spiritual realm beyond what my undisciplined and immature spiritual life had prepared me for, but, oh, how ardently I longed to stay there! It was far more painful to return to everyday life and know I had to make an effort to live it for many more years. The transition was like using a limb that has been comfortably paralysed by cold until it thaws out. I came gradually through the process of mourning to live again an ordinary life and return to work, social life and so on, with no spiritual or other-worldly experiences for some years.

Perhaps the most useful thing I can say is that these 'experiences' (not all are clear-cut and obvious, some are uncertain and shade into everyday life) *cannot* be 'evaluated' in the same way as other mental states of experience, because they have the quality of being not only self-authenticating but being the ground or standard by which everything else in my subjective experience can be, and is, judged. This phenomenon itself is not unknown in abnormal states of delusion and hallucination but is not as common in them as might be supposed, and, in my experience, invariably leads to progressive mental deterioration, pain and, eventually, psychological and social disintegration, whereas the only objective test of spiritual experiences is that they show fruit in enhanced sensitivity and maturity, and lead to growth in all areas of the personality.

However strange these experiences are, they are firmly incarnational, in being mediated through blood and bone, nerve cell, imagination and the memory store of individual experience. There is also the paradox that although, on the one hand, these are the most significant things in my life and probably the most enduring, in that they do not seem to fade like memories of ordinary experiences, yet I know that in my Christian life they are somehow the least important – one of the means by which the spirit calls my attention and then works on me, one contribution I make to the corporate body of the Church, but certainly not more valuable than my simple presence at worship on Sunday or the least Christian service I give to others.

CONTINUOUS AWARENESS

*

Among the accounts were a very few letters from people who do not describe a particular experience, but a continuous awareness of some other factor in their lives. We have selected three of these accounts only. They speak of an awareness of a 'power'. It seemed relevant to include these accounts precisely because they show a different aspect of this subject.

There may be many people who have a lifelong awareness of a power or powers beyond themselves, but the questions in articles and magazines asked for 'experiences' and 'events'. The fact that nevertheless a few people responded with these types of account shows that *they* consider them as significant enough to record them.

F. 75   139

Since childhood I have been *aware* of a great Power outside us,
calling for awe and for concern for others with whom this Power
links us.

I am 75 now, and even when I did not open the little cell of my
life to this never-failing flow of Life – Love – Power, I knew it was
waiting to be 'drawn on'. As the years have gone by, I have become
more and more conscious of THIS being the central spark of life
in us. That we are little cells receiving and transmitting this Life of
Love, if we are willing to open our 'valves'. There is nothing vague
about this circulation of divine love within and around us. One
recognizes what are something like personal (supra-personal, perhaps I should say) relationships between our little cells of human
life, and this fullness of Life and Love which transcends any words
or images we could think up.

I have been, am, writing this in an open ward of a hospital these
last weeks – *never has THIS PRESENCE been more intimate and
powerful*.

I have never had visionary or auditory hallucinations, but varieties
of recognized experiences with higher Powers or Beings and One
who enfolds us all.

F. ?   1139

Since about the age of 6 I have had an awareness of a higher
power. At all times I am aware of this power, which is as real to me
as any in the physical world. In this sense, I live in two spheres of
influence.

When I am tranquil, as in bed late at night, I place my problems
before this higher power and I am shown the way to solve them.

Apart from problems, I open my mind to this higher power and
I obtain peace and happiness of a kind not normally associated with
the physical world.

Foreshadowings of world and other events are sometimes given
to me. These events are not necessarily personal to me, except
incidentally. I do not search for prophecy, as it is usually best to
live in the present and not burden oneself.

I avoid all trance conditions. I am not a spiritualist.

Through being as I am it seems to me that I am protected in life.

One cannot satisfactorily state one's experiences, especially in a letter. Firstly, they are too varied. Secondly, language is inadequate for this.

Originally a Catholic, since 12 I have belonged to no organized religion whatsoever. I belong to no group.

I should add that I am a very practical person. I now operate holiday accommodation.

M. ?   4629

I recently read an article about 'sudden blinding convictions of "being watched over"' that 'everything is "all right"'. In my case those feelings have arisen, and strongly so, not from a sudden blinding conviction, but rather from an overwhelming accumulation of incidents, many of them trifling, almost daily over the past couple of years or so. This has given me the impression that God is looking after me in the minutest particulars; I find it incredible but I'm getting a bit more used to it now!

I was recently made redundant after twenty-six years service and obtained my present job, without a break, through a remarkable chain of fifteen 'links', the breaking of any one of which would have meant I would not have got the post, I and which are eminently suited to each other. By about the twelfth link I developed an overwhelming feeling of being led by divine providence, regardless of whether the end was to be success in getting the job or not.

One other aspect is the feeling that I have yet to fulfil my main purpose (whatever it may prove to be) of my life and that the past two years have been an advanced stage on the path along which, not far ahead now, that purpose will be revealed to me. This tallies with my perception that this, initially daily, attention to my minor needs is a way of building up my confidence, assurance, faith (call it what you will) to meet whatever demands are going to be made upon me.

The word which best describes the whole development is awesome; not frightening, but exciting, fascinating, even fun, quite encouraging but, mostly, awesome – as of an irresistible but supportive power.

Glossary

*

This glossary is intended to provide guidance to the meanings of some of the words used in this book. It does not claim to be authoritative or definitive.

awareness: a state of being aware, consciousness in an indefinable way.

clairvoyance, clair-audience: the ability to see or hear things not present to the senses.

contemplation: an aspect of meditation; to gaze upon; devotion to.

conversion: a religious turning point, often experienced as dramatic and life-changing.

déjà vu: literally, 'already seen'; sense of 'I have been here before'.

ecstasy: a state of altered consciousness, of being 'out of one's self' (not physically), usually experienced as rapturous or joyful, and as if coming from a somehow-spiritual source.

experience: (a) *an* experience, a direct acquaintance with something by mind, feeling or perception; having the quality of immediacy; (b) experience – events or life passed through.

extra-sensory perception (ESP): literally, 'perceiving outside the senses'; having the faculties of clairvoyance, clairaudience, telepathy or precognition.

hypnosis: a sleeplike state in which the mind is responsive to suggestion and can recall the forgotten past.

ineffable: beyond description; words cannot describe.

inspiration: a feeling of being prompted by God or by an idea or a feeling.

instinct: an inborn tendency to certain acts without conscious will or impulse; an unconscious skill.

intuition: a 'hunch', insight, 'sixth sense'; perceives wholes; not an act of judgement.

levitation: an act of rising in the air, sometimes spiritually caused.

medium: a person through whom contact is made with the spirits of the dead and with the spirit world generally.

mysticism: a conviction of the mysterious unity at the heart of all things, leading to world-wide religious and other practices seeking to experience this unity.

near-death experience: feeling drawn towards a region of light and love, often as if travelling along a tunnel; sometimes all life passes before; experienced by people who may have seemed physically dead; nearly always followed by loss of fear of death.

numinous: pertaining to a divinity; describes a sense of the divine, of a godhead, of the holy.

out-of-body experience: the conscious self seems to leave the body and locate itself outside, often near the ceiling, while retaining the ability to observe its own body and events surrounding it.

paranormal: 'facts' that do not fit into the ways in which we conceive and explain the everyday world.

parapsychology (or Psi, or ESP research): the study of such things as telepathy and clairvoyance, which seems to suggest that we can gain knowledge by means other than our normal modes of perception.

peak experience: an ecstatic experience similar to the religious mystical unitive experience, but triggered by situations such as love, dancing, childbirth, sex, aesthetic insight, etc.

precognition: knowing of an event or circumstance before it happens; a faculty of ESP (see above).

psychic: concerned with paranormal cognition (ESP) (see above).

psychosis: a mental disorder, characterized in part by lack of insight into his own condition on the part of the patient.

quietism: a form of religious mysticism; passive devotional contemplation (see above); calmness and passivity.

schizophrenia: a form of psychosis, an inability to distinguish reality from unreality, sometimes characterized in part by hallucinations.

spiritualism: philosophically, the doctrine that the spirit has real existence apart from matter; in practice, the interpretation of mediumistic contact with spirits.

synchronicity: patterning of events; not necessarily a religious experience.

telepathy: the transmission of ideas from one mind to another by means other than the use of ordinary physical senses; a faculty of ESP (see above).

transcendence: that which is perceived or experienced beyond the limits of normal perception, including the possibility of divinity.

transcendent: beyond the limits of normal perception.

trigger: antecedent; occasion; object, event or idea immediately prior to an experience.

References

*

The Alister Hardy Research Centre

1 A. Hardy, *The Spiritual Nature of Man*, Oxford, Oxford University Press, 1979, p.18.
2 *Observer*, 8 March 1970.
3 W. James, *The Varieties of Religious Experience*, New York, Longman Green & Co., 1902, and London, Collins, 1960.
4 ibid. p. 501.
5 B. P. Brennan, *William James*, New York, Twayne Publishers Inc., 1968, p. 100.
6 Hardy, op. cit., p. 23.
7 E. Robinson, *The Original Vision*, New York, The Seabury Press, 1983.
8 T. Beardsworth, *A Sense of Presence*, Oxford, Religious Experience Reasearch Unit, 1977.
9 D. Hay, *Exploring Inner Space*, Oxford, Mowbray, 1987.
10 James, op. cit., p. 25.
11 R. D. Laing, *The Politics of Experience*, London, Penguin, 1967.
12 A. Storr, *Jung*, London, Collins, 1986.

An Introduction to Transcendent Experience

1 N. Smart, *The Religious Experience of Humankind*, London, Collins, 1971.
2 Exodus 3:1–15.
3 Lion Handbook, *The World's Religions*, Tring, Lion Publishing Co., 1982, p. 224.
4 Luke 1:26–28; 2:9–14.
5 Matthew 3:17.
6 Mark 1:13.
7 *The Koran*, trs. N. J. Dawood, Harmondsworth, Penguin, 1956, p. 9.
8 G. K. Chesterton, *Saint Francis of Assisi*, New York, Doubleday, 1924, p. 50.
9 Julian of Norwich, *Revelations of Divine Love*, trs. Clifton Wolters, Harmondsworth, Penguin, 1966, p. 63.

10 Julian of Norwich, *Enfolded in Love*, London, Darton, Longman & Todd, 1980, p. 15.

11 *Brewer's Dictionary of Phrase and Fable*, Second (revised) edn., London, Cassell, 1981, p. 36.

12 E. Robinson (ed.), *This Timebound Ladder*, Oxford, Religious Experience Research Unit, 1977, p. 29.

13 ibid. p. 48.

14 R. Otto, *The Idea of the Holy*, trs. John W. Harvey, Oxford, Oxford University Press, 1950.

15 W. Johnston, *The Inner Eye of Love*, London, Collins, 1978, p. 47.

16 A. H. Maslow, *Religions, Values and Peak-Experiences*, Harmondsworth, Penguin, 1964.

17 W. James, *The Varieties of Religious Experience*, New York, Longman Green & Co., 1902, and London, Collins, 1960, p. 489.

18 M. Laski, *Ecstasy*, London, Cresset Press, 1961.

19 James, op. cit., p. 367.

20 E. Robinson, *The Original Vision*, New York, Seabury Press, 1983.

21 Luke 1:29–30.

22 Matthew 14:26-end; Luke 24:5.

23 G. Parrinder, *Mysticism in the World's Religions*, London, Sheldon Press, 1976, p. 13.

24 E. Robinson (ed.), *Living the Questions*, Oxford, Religious Experience Research Unit, 1978, pp. 30–31.

25 James, op. cit., p. 367.

26 John 6:35; 8:12; 8:58.

27 R. A. Moody, *Life after Life*, New York, Bantam, 1975, pp. 34–55.

28 W. Y. Evans-Wentz (ed.), *The Tibetan Book of the Dead*, Oxford, Oxford University Press, 1960, p. 18.

29 C. G. Jung, *Memories, Dreams, Reflections*, London, Collins, 1963, p. 341.

30 G. Aurora, 'Studying "Religious Experience" in India', unpublished paper, undated.

31 1 Samuel 3:1–14.

32 James, op. cit., p. 367.

33 Julian of Norwich, *Enfolded in Love*, London, Darton, Longman & Todd, 1980, p. 15.

34 D. Hay, *Exploring Inner Space*, Oxford, Mowbray, 1987, p. 174.

35 J. Ashton, personal communication, 1988.

36 Maslow, op. cit., p. 67.

37 Julian of Norwich, *Enfolded in Love*, London, Darton, Longman & Todd, 1980, p. 39.

38 Maslow, op. cit., p. 67.

39 Matthew 18:3.
40 V. Frankl, *Man's Search for Meaning*, London, Hodder & Stoughton, 1962.

Articles and Appeals

Over the years there have been many appeals made and articles written by and on behalf of the AHRC. The following list of some of the titles is by no means exhaustive. Some articles could not be traced and the information on some others is not complete. They are listed here in order of date of appearance.

New Christian, 1 April 1969.
'Exploring the World of the Spirit', *The Times*, 7 and 28 March 1970.
'Supernatural Selection', *Observer Colour Supplement*, 8 March 1970.
Auckland Star, 1970.
'Have you ever believed in God?', *Daily Mail*, 28 July 1971.
Science Digest, September 1971.
Daily Mail, September 1971.
Thames Television, 19 January 1972.
'God is more than real', *Home Words*, February 1972.
Windsor Parish Magazine, March 1972.
Psychic, September 1972.
'Is there really a God?', *Manchester Evening News*, 8 November 1972.
'A Scientist Looks at Religion', (television), 9 August 1973.
'It could happen to you', *Everyman* (BBC TV), January 1980.
'In Search of Miracles', *Fate*, August 1983.
'In Perspective', BBC Radio 4, 13 October 1984.
'Computers on the road to Damascus', *Sunday Times*, 14 October 1984.
'Research into Spiritual Experiences', *The Methodist Recorder*, 18 October 1984.
Church Times, 19 October 1984.
Baptist Times, 25 October 1984.
The Friend, 26 October 1984.
Catholic Herald, 28 October 1984.
'Scientists find God', *The War Cry*, 3 November 1984.
The Listener, 17 November 1984.
Irish radio, December 1984.
'Join the Paras', *Woman*, 12 January 1985.
'You Unlimited', *Vogue*, February 1985.
'Catching an Angel in a Net', *Time*, 11 March 1985.

Further Reading

*

Ahern, G., *Spiritual/Religious Experience in Modern Society*, 1990, (available at AHRC Oxford).

Argyle, M., *Religious Behaviour*, London, Routledge & Kegan Paul, 1958.

Batson, C. P. & Ventis, L. W., *The Religious Experience*, Oxford, Oxford University Press, 1982.

Beardsworth, T., *A Sense of Presence*, Oxford, Religious Experience Research Unit, 1977.

Bodkin, M., *Archetypal Patterns in Poetry*, Oxford, Oxford University Press, 1974.

Boison, A. T., *The Exploration of the Inner World: a study of mental disorder and religious experience*, New York, Harper Torchbooks, n.d.

Brennan, B. P., *William James*, New York, Twayne Publishers Inc., 1968.

Brown, L. D. (ed.), *Advances on the Psychology of Religion*, Oxford, Pergamon Press, 1985.

Clark, J. H., *A Map of Mental States*, London, Routledge & Kegan Paul, 1983.

Clark, W. H., *Chemical Ecstasy: psychedelic drugs and religion*, Kansas City, Mo., Andrews & McMeel, 1962.

Cohen, J. M. & Phipps, J-F., *The Common Experience*, London, Rider, 1979.

Coxhead, N., *The Relevance of Bliss*, London, Wildwood House Ltd, 1985.

Crookall, B., *The Interpretation of Cosmic and Mystical Experiences*, Cambridge & London, James Clark & Co., 1969.

Crookall, R., *The Jung-Jaffé View of Out-of-the-Body Experiences*, Los Angeles, World Fellowship Press, 1970.

Durkheim, E., *The Elementary Forms of the Religious Life*, London, Allen & Unwin, 1976.

Eliade, M., *From Primitives to Zen*, London, Collins, 1967.

Fay, W. (ed.), *Man's Religious Quest: a reader*, London, Croom Helm, 1978.

Freud, S., *New Introductory Lectures on Psycho-analysis, Vol 2.*, Harmondsworth, Penguin, 1973.

Greeley, A. M., *Ecstasy: a Way of Knowing*, Englewood Cliffs, N.J., Prentice-Hall, n.d.

Harding, R. E. M., *An Anatomy of Inspiration*, Cambridge, W. Heffer & Sons, 1967.

Hardy, Sir Alister, *The Divine Flame*, London, Collins, 1966.

Hardy, Sir Alister, *The Spiritual Nature of Man*, Oxford, Oxford University Press, 1984.

Hay, D., *Exploring Inner Space*, Oxford, Mowbrays, 1987.

Huxley, A., *The Perennial Philosophy*, London, Chatto & Windus, 1946.

Huxley, A., *The Doors of Perception*, London, Chatto & Windus, 1954.

James, W., *The Varieties of Religious Experience*, Harmondsworth, Penguin Books, 1960.

Johnson, R. C., *The Imprisoned Splendour*, London, Hodder & Stoughton, 1953.

Johnson, R. C.. *Watcher on the Hills*, London, Hodder & Stoughton, 1959.

Johnson, W., *The Inner Eye of Love (Mysticism and Religion)*, London, Collins, 1978.

Jonas, H., *The Gnostic Religion*, Boston, Beacon Press, 1985.

Jung, C. G., *The Archetypes and the Collective Unconscious*, London, Routledge & Kegan Paul, 1971.

Katz, S. T. (ed.), *Mysticism and Philosophical Analysis*, New York, Oxford University Press, 1978.

Kelsey, Morton, *The Christian and the Supernatural*, London, Search Press, 1977.

Laski, M., *Ecstasy*, London, Cresset Press, 1961.

Laski, M., *Everyday Ecstasy*, London, Thames & Hudson, 1980.

Lello, R. S. (ed.), *Revelations, Glimpses of Reality*, London, Shepheard-Walwyn (Publishers) Ltd, 1985.

LeShan, L., *The Medium, the Mystic & the Physicist*, New York, Viking Press, 1974.

LeShan, L., *Science of the Paranormal*, Wellingborough, Aquarian Press, 1987.

Maslow, A., *Towards a Psychology of Being*, Princeton, N.J., Van Nostrand Co. Inc., 1962.

Maslow, A. H., *Religions, Values and Peak-Experiences*, Harmondsworth, Penguin, 1964.

Moody, R., *Life After Life*, New York, Bantam Books, 1976.

Moody, R., *Reflections on Life After Life*, London, Bantam Books, 1978.

Murti, T. R. V., *The Central Philosophy of Buddhism*, London, Unwin Paperbacks, 1980.

Pafford, M., *Inglorious Wordsworths*, London, Hodder & Stoughton, 1973.

Parrinder, G., *Mysticism in the World's Religions*, London, Sheldon Press, 1976.

Ring, K., *Heading Towards Omega: in search of the meaning of the Near-Death Experience*, New York, William Morrow, 1984.

Robinson, E. (ed.), *This Timebound Ladder*, Oxford, Religious Experience Research Unit, 1977.

Robinson, E., *Living the Questions*, Oxford, Religious Experience Research Unit, 1978.

Robinson, E., *The Original Vision*, New York, Seabury Press, 1984.

Sheldrake, R., *A New Science of Life*, London, Collins, 1981.

Sheldrake, R., *The Presence of the Past*, London, Collins, 1988.

Smart, N., *The Religious Experience of Mankind*, London, Collins, 1971.

Smart, N., *Concept and Empathy*, London, Macmillan, 1986.

Stace, W. T., *Mysticism and Philosophy*, Philadelphia, Lippincott, 1960.

Stael, F., *Exploring Mysticism*, Harmondsworth, Penguin Books, 1980.

Starbuck, E., *The Psychology of Religion*, London, Walter Scott, n.d.

Storr, A., *Jung*, London, Collins, 1986.

Underhill, E., *Mysticism: a study in the nature and development of man's spiritual consciousness*, London, Methuen, 1957.

Zaehner, R. C., *Mysticism, Sacred & Profane*, Oxford, Oxford University Press, 1980.

General Index

*

Agnostic(ism), 25, 54, 84, 113, 116, 188
Ahern, G., 8
Alister Hardy, 5, 6, 8
Alister Hardy Research Centre, (AHRC), 1–9, 15, 23, 26–7, 30, 40, 45
'All will be well', 38, 62, 80, 128, 154, 163, 187
Alone, 40, 47, 52, 75, 100, 109, 120, 133, 134, 151, 156, 171
Altruism, 57, 195
Angel(s), 11, 20, 28, 30, 34, 71, 91, 112, 164, 172, 191
   guardian angel, 34, 143
Arrested, 126, 127
Art, painting, 15, 46, 107
Atheist(s), 76, 104, 108
Atman, 112
Aware(ness), 5, 15, 24, 32, 58, 90, 103, 138, 197
   continuous, 194–6; heightened, 24
Awe, awesome, 46, 51, 57, 141, 150, 151, 153, 168, 195–6

Background,
   cultural, 21; religious, 21
Beardsworth, T., 6
Bed,
   in/on bed, 75, 84, 93, 101, 109, 112, 118, 120, 129, 163, 164, 172, 177, 179, 184, 195; bedside, 72, 90, 122; foot of the b., 96, 114
Being, 24, 25, 52, 61, 104, 107, 112, 154, 165
   not-being, 36, 107
Belief,
   in a supreme being, 49; in Christ, 122; in God, 67, 82, 97, 134, 144
Bible, 20, 59, 84, 117, 146

training, 59; reading, 84; new translation of, 117; Gideon B., 84
Birth (labour), 26, 56, 60, 66, 95, 126
Blake, W., 174
Blasphemy, 56
Bliss(ful), 53, 92, 110
Body,
   left my body, 64–5; trapped in the b., 128; out of b. 138; filled my b., 177
   see also Out of body experience
Born again, 102
   reborn, 119
Boulding, K., 126–7
Breakthrough, 8, 91–2
Browning, R., 48
Buddha, Buddhist,
   culture, 9; the B. Siddharta Gautama, 11; under the Bo-tree, 41

Certainty, 37, 38, 81, 95, 102, 187
   absolute, 94; perfect assurance, 97; indwelling, 98
   see also Knowledge
Change, 20, 31–40, 51, 96, 102, 117, 120, 126, 144, 155
   life-changing, 6, 81, 84, 85, 88, 95, 99, 103, 119, 113, 137, 140, 172, 177, 185
   no doubt now, 89; everything in a new light, 114; body changing, 179; renewal, 184; growth, 193
Chanting, 8
Child, 42, 81, 87, 180
   childhood, 6, 7, 19, 180; adolescence, 81
Christ, see Jesus
Christian(ity), 33, 35, 41, 76, 92
Christian Church,

evil, 158; of a person, 160; of an
authority, 160–1; of people, 170;
of husband, 177
Prison, 32, 36, 54
Profundity, 138
Prophet, 10
prophetic experience, 15, 16, 59
Psychic,
experience, 15, 26; forces, 34;
faculties, 124; artist, 165
Psychology, depth psychology, 5
reality, 5; trauma, 57; terrifying, 61;
psychologist, 88
Psychotherapy, 27, 41
Psychosis, psychotic, 7, 8, 27
ended, 87–8; experience, 172
Purpose (of religious or transcendent
experience), 39–40

Quaker(s), 54, 55
Society of Friends, 62, 127, 169

Rahere, 11–12
Raphael, Archangel, 113
Real, reality, 14, 17, 18, 21, 24, 42, 50,
56–7, 61, 81, 151, 154, 161, 178
of God, 38, 55, 81, 103, 119, 138;
r. person, 41; another r., 42;
spiritual r., 43; physical r., 43;
ultimate r., 62; of Jesus, 104; more
r. than r., 107; r. time, 111
Religion, religious,
interest in, 47; no interest in, 84;
very r. woman, 92; not a r. fanatic,
144; doubts about Christian r.,
188
see also Experience
'Remembering', 41
Revelation(s), 10, 24, 101, 108, 136
Reverence, a sense of, 4
Ritual,
burial, 10; need for, 13
Robinson, E., 23

Sai Baba, 87
Saint(s), 28, 30, 34
St Bartholomew, 11–12; St Francis
of Assisi, 41; St John, 55; St Paul,
41, 183; St Theresa, 102,
179–180; St Thomas, 168
Samuel (prophet), 36
Sane, 63

Self,
loss of, 28; beyond the, 41;
subconscious, 118; self-
authenticating experiencing, 193
Senses,
seeing, 28, see also Nature, Figure,
Lights; hearing, 28, 30, see also
Voice; touch/sensation, 28, 30, 73,
76–7, 80, 83, 89, 92, 96, 98,
101–2 see also Touch; smell, 28,
72, 192; taste, 28
Sex
the great taboo, 190
Smell,
perfume, 58; of flowers, 71–2;
fragrance of ripe grapes, 109;
fragrance, 133; scent of pines, 192
Song,
stars singing, 64
Soubirous, B., 13
Sound,
wind-like, 112; monotonous, 133;
gentle, 176
Spiral(ing) 50, 92
Spiritual,
awareness, 6; spirituality, 8–9;
direction, 41; spiritually
intermingled, 42; world, 42;
creature, 156
Stace, W. T., 5
Starbuck, E., 5
Stress (distress), 146, 156
state of, 29–31; physical distress, 29;
trouble, 31; anguish, 31;
desperation, 31, 145;
psychological, 31; deep distress,
37, 146, 156; times of, 39;
confused, 147; scared stiff, 147;
despair, 186; desolated, 192
Suicide(s),
thinking of . . . suicide, 67; suicides
in Jonestown, 159
Synchronicity, 33, 197
Symbol,
a morning glory flower, 61

Taboo, 16–17, 52, 56, 62, 74, 108,
138, 150, 158, 187
Telepathy, 17, 33, 113, 197
Tibetan Book of the Dead, 27
Time,
concept of, 18; stood still, 47;

Index of Reference Numbers

*

139	p. 195	2476	p. 162	3144	p. 175
143	145	2479	93	3191	158
248	70	2495	95	3401	134
322	46	2496	91	3670	156
398	67	2497	80	4056	86
446	87	2498	121	4057	74
583	173	2505	108	4063	177
630	67	2524	77	4067	112
639	100	2526	102	4071	127
640	76	2530	98	4091	102
657	115	2547	178	4092	81
874	150	2552	108	4103	177
904	133	2562	101	4104	93
947	59	2563	92	4107	116
1131	88	2565	95	4110	68
1133	46	2568	144	4113	137
1136	54	2596	100	4114	75
1139	195	2602	164	4123	87
1143	153	2604	125	4127	184
1145	181	2611	64	4136	127
1239	47	2643	144	4138	55
1284	48	2657	141	4182	61
1531	146	2668	134	4185	183
1637	116	2676	166	4217	128
2009	147	2674	72	4230	73
2010	81	2720	79	4232	185
2011	119	2723	94	4233	126
2012	79	2726	122	4284	130
2026	72	2733	66	4267	56
2035	49	2772	129	4278	62
2049	94	2848	52	4281	93
2062	73	3006	121	4315	90
2072	138	3009	97	4325	69
2074	160	3015	78	4327	147
2138	63	3020	143	4332	140
2366	49	3062	137	4340	118
2461	136	3088	99	4350	120